# STUFF! GOOD PIANO PLAYERS SHOULD KNOW

## AN A to Z GUIDE TO GETTING BETTER

### Take your playing from ordinary to EXTRAORDINARY!

by Mark Harrison

ISBN 978-1-4234-2781-0

HAL•LEONARD® CORPORATION

7777 W. BLUEMOUND RD. P.O. BOX 13819 MILWAUKEE, WI 53213

In Australia Contact:
**Hal Leonard Australia Pty. Ltd.**
4 Lentara Court
Cheltenham, Victoria, 3192 Australia
Email: ausadmin@halleonard.com.au

Visit Hal Leonard Online at
**www.halleonard.com**

# CONTENTS

# INTRODUCTION

Welcome to *Stuff! Good Piano Players Should Know*. This book-and-CD package is chock full of techniques and tricks to help your playing become more professional. Just dive into the alphabetical list of tips to learn what you need to know, from styles (blues, boogie-woogie, funk, gospel, jazz, rock, and more) to piano techniques (arpeggios, crossover licks, left-hand patterns, neighbor tones, target notes, and more) to music theory (diatonic chords, triads, seventh chords, downbeats and upbeats, voice leading, and more)... you get the idea!

Good luck with playing your stuff on the piano!

—Mark Harrison

# ABOUT THE CD

On the accompanying CD, you'll find recordings of almost all the musical examples in the book. Most of the tracks feature a full band, with the rhythm section on the left channel and the piano on the right channel. To play along with the band on these tracks, simply turn down the right channel. The solo piano tracks feature the left-hand piano part on the left channel, and the right-hand piano part on the right channel, for easy hands-separate practice as needed.

# ABOUT THE AUTHOR

Mark Harrison studied classical piano as a child, and by his teenage years was playing in various rock bands in his native Southern England. In the 1980s he began writing music for TV and commercials, including a piece that was used for the British Labor Party ads in a national election. He also appeared on British television (BBC), and became a fixture on London's pub-rock circuit.

In 1987 he relocated to Los Angeles to experience the music business in the U.S.A. He soon began performing with top musicians such as Jay Graydon (Steely Dan), John Molo (Bruce Hornsby band), Jimmy Haslip (Yellowjackets), and numerous others. Mark currently performs with his own contemporary jazz band (the Mark Harrison Quintet), as well as with the Steely Dan tribute band Doctor Wu. His recent TV music credits include *Saturday Night Live, The Montel Williams Show, American Justice, Celebrity Profiles, America's Most Wanted, True Hollywood Stories*, the British documentary program *Panorama*, and many others.

Mark is also one of the top contemporary music educators in Los Angeles. He taught at the renowned Grove School of Music for six years, instructing hundreds of musicians from all around the world. Mark currently runs a busy private teaching studio, catering to the needs of professional and amateur musicians alike. His students include GRAMMY®-winners, hit songwriters, members of the Boston Pops and Los Angeles Philharmonic orchestras, and first-call touring musicians with major acts.

Mark's music instruction books are used by thousands of musicians in over twenty countries, and are recommended by the Berklee College of Music for all their new students. Mark also writes master-class articles covering a variety of styles and topics for *Keyboard* and *How to Jam* magazines. Please visit Mark at **www.harrisonmusic.com** for information about his educational products and services, as well as his live performance activities and schedule.

## ADD9 CHORDS

*Adding ninths* (sometimes referred to as seconds) is a great way to spice up major and minor chords in pop and rock styles. The ninth is the highest extension in a five-part chord—for example, a Cmaj9 chord would be spelled C-E-G-B-D, so D would be the ninth. However, in contemporary styles we will often want to add the ninth but exclude the seventh, which is what the chord symbol C(add9) is telling us to do. The ninth is often played (or voiced) a whole step above the root of the chord, which is why it is sometimes called a second. Let's see how to apply the add9 chords to some comping patterns.

TRACK 1

Pop ballad – basic triads

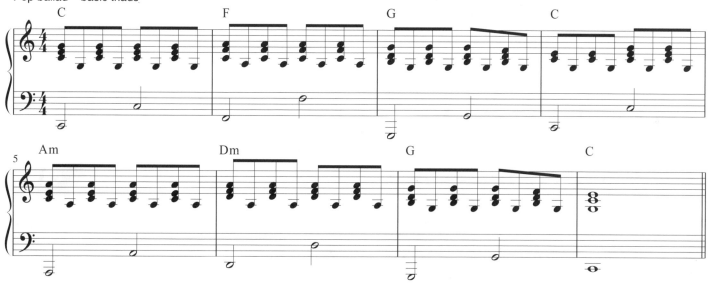

Notice that we are just using simple major or minor triads in the right hand, with voice leading (inverting the triads to move smoothly between successive chords) and octave doubling (duplicating the top note of the right hand an octave lower). As in most piano ballad styles, we depress the sustain pedal for the duration of each chord. This groove uses an alternating-eighths right-hand technique (alternating between the chords played on the downbeats, and the thumb notes played in between on the upbeats). Now we'll vary this pattern by adding ninths to the chords.

TRACK 2

Pop ballad – triads with added 9ths

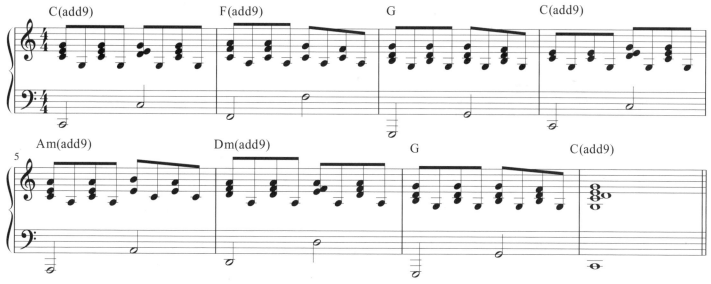

Notice that the ninth often moves (or resolves) to the root of the chord—the movement from D to C in measure 1, for example. Although the chord symbols have been upgraded to reflect the added ninths, in practice you'll often apply this technique to chord charts with only basic triad chord symbols (when stylistically appropriate, of course). Next we'll look at a pop/rock comping pattern.

TRACK 3

Pop/rock – basic triads

Again, we are using basic major and minor triads, with voice leading. In this pop/rock style, the right hand is playing a steady driving eighth-note rhythmic pattern, and the left hand is playing the root of each chord, with an anticipation (landing an eighth note ahead) of beat 3 in each measure. Now we'll upgrade this pattern with added ninths.

TRACK 4

Pop/rock with added 9ths

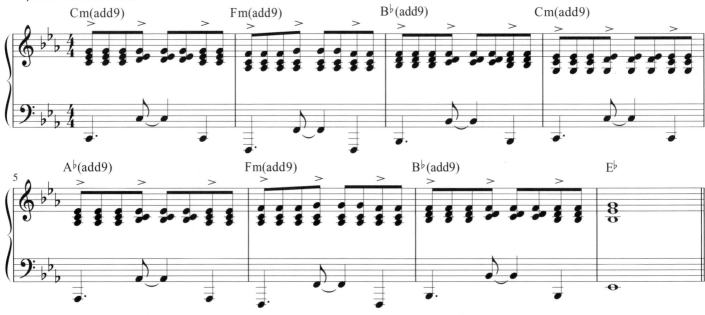

Again, notice how the ninth resolves to the root of each chord (i.e., the motion from D to C in measure 1). Have fun with your added ninths. As with any harmonic device, don't overdo it; but in the right context, it will make your piano parts sound very hip!

# ALTERNATING EIGHTH NOTES

*Alternating eighths* is a term I use to describe a comping style where the right hand alternates between the upper notes of a chord (played with the 2nd, 3rd, 4th, and/or 5th fingers) and the lowest note of that chord (played with the thumb), using an eighth-note rhythmic pattern. We saw some examples of this technique in *Add9 Chords* (p. 5), employed in a pop ballad style. Next we'll apply this concept to a pop/rock shuffle groove.

TRACK 5

Note the "swing-eighths" symbol above the music (telling you to treat each pair of eighth notes as a quarter-eighth triplet): this is how we create the shuffle feel for this example. Listen to the CD track to make sure you're comfortable with this swing-eighths rhythmic subdivision. Also, in this groove both the right- and left-hand parts are anticipating beat 3 (landing an eighth note before the beat).

## CHORD VOICING TIPS

This is our first example using upper-structure triads, a vital voicing technique in many contemporary styles. The right-hand notes on the Cm7 chords form an E♭ major triad (E♭-G-B♭). These are the third, fifth, and seventh of the Cm7 chord, and can be thought of as a major triad (E♭ major in this case) built from the third of the chord (Cm7 in this case). In a similar fashion, an F major triad has been built from the third of all the Dm7 chords.

We've also used a couple of different upper structures on the major chords. On the E♭maj7 chords, the right-hand notes form a G minor triad (giving us the third, fifth, and seventh of the E♭maj7 chord), a minor triad built from the third of the chord. On the B♭maj7 chord, the right-hand notes form an F major triad (the fifth, seventh, and ninth of the B♭maj7 chord), a major triad built from the fifth of the chord. This upgrades the chord symbol by adding the ninth (and removing the third), giving a transparent, modern sound.

The F11 chord is a suspended dominant, where the fourth or eleventh has replaced the third. For this we have built a major triad from the seventh of the chord (E♭ in this case), giving us the seventh, ninth, and eleventh of the chord. The Dsus2 chord indicates that we have replaced the third of a D major triad with the second (or ninth). The resulting voicing in the last measure can be thought of as an inversion of a double 4th, which is a three-note shape built using intervals of a 4th (here E-A-D). We'll return to these very hip double-4th voicings later!

7

TRACK 6

Our next alternating-eighths pattern is in a basic country style, played with straight eighths.

Basic country

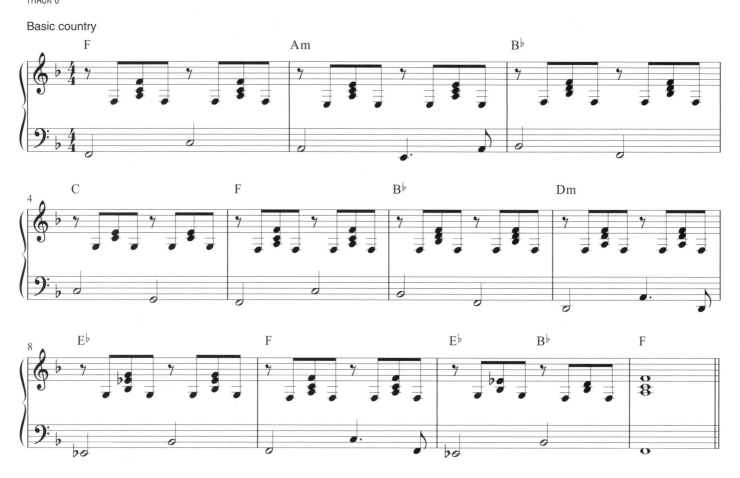

Here the right hand plays a triad on beats 2 and 4 of each measure, alternating with the thumb note (an octave below the top note of each triad) on each upbeat. Note that the left hand plays on beats 1 and 3 (moving from the root to the fifth of each chord), while the right hand rests on these beats; this creates the back-and-forth motion between the hands that is typical of country comping styles. The right-hand part is voiced with basic major and minor triads derived from the chord symbols, using inversions to voice lead smoothly through the progression.

## ANTICIPATIONS

An *anticipation* occurs when a rhythmic event lands before the beat, and is then held over (or followed by a rest on) the beat. An example of an eighth-note anticipation would be a chord landing on an upbeat (say, halfway through beat 2) and then holding through the following downbeat (beat 3 in this case). The pop/rock shuffle groove of **Track 5** (p. 7) is a good example of this. An example of a sixteenth-note anticipation would be a chord landing on the last sixteenth note within the beat, and then held through the following beat. Here we will focus on sixteenth-note anticipations, beginning with an R&B ballad.

TRACK 7

R&B ballad

Note how the right-hand voicings are often anticipating (landing a sixteenth note ahead of) beat 3. Also, the left-hand pattern frequently anticipates beats 2 and/or 4. This all combines to create a rhythmic conversation between the hands that is typical of R&B ballad styles.

## CHORD VOICING TIPS

This R&B ballad example also uses upper-structure triads and four-part chord shapes as follows:

- The Bm7 and Gm7 chords are voiced by building major triads from the third: D/B and B♭/G.

- The A11 chord in measure 6 is voiced by building a major triad from the seventh: G/A.

- The Dmaj9 and B♭maj9 chords are voiced by building minor-seventh shapes from the third: F♯m7/D and Dm7/B♭.

- The A11 chord in measure 10 is voiced by building a minor-seventh shape from the fifth: Em7/A.

- The A7♭9 chord is voiced by building a diminished-seventh shape from the third: C♯dim7/A.

We also have some added ninths on the major chords in measures 2 and 3. And the left hand is using some root-fifth, root-seventh, and open-triad arpeggio patterns.

The next example uses anticipations within a swing-sixteenths rhythmic framework, often found in today's funk shuffle and hip-hop styles. Note the "swing-sixteenths" symbol above the music (telling you to treat each pair of sixteenth notes as an eighth-sixteenth triplet); again, check out the CD track to get comfortable with this rhythmic feel. The right-hand voicings are often anticipating beat 1 by a sixteenth note, which together with the down-beats used in the left-hand part (whole notes in measures 1–4, and quarter-note octaves from measure 5 onward) is characteristic of funk piano styles.

**TRACK 8**

R&B/funk shuffle

## CHORD VOICING TIPS

This R&B/funk shuffle example also uses upper-structure triads and four-part chord shapes as follows:

- The G7 chords are voiced by building a diminished triad from the third: Bdim/G.
- The C11 and F11 chords are voiced by building major triads from the seventh: B♭/C and E♭/F.

- The Cm7 chord is voiced by building a major triad from the third: E♭/C.

- The G11 chords are voiced by building a minor-seventh shape from the fifth: Dm7/G.

- The D7(♯5,♭9) chords are voiced by building a minor-seventh-flatted-fifth shape from the seventh: Cm7♭5/D.

- The D7(♯5,♯9) chords are voiced by building a major-seventh-flatted-fifth shape from the third: F♯maj7♭5/D.

- The E♭maj9 chord is voiced by building a minor-seventh shape from the third: Gm7/E♭.

On the G7 chords (as well as the B diminished triads), we are also adding some passing triads (C major and D minor). These come from the G Mixolydian mode.

# ARPEGGIOS

**TRACK 9**

An *arpeggio* is the result of playing the notes of a chord one at a time, or "broken chord" style. This technique has many applications in both classical and popular music. Our first example is an excerpt from Mozart's Piano Sonata in C Major, which uses an arpeggio accompaniment in the left hand below the melody in the right hand.

In the first measure, the left-hand notes C-G-E-G outline a C major triad. In the second measure, the left-hand notes D-G-F-G (together with the B in the right-hand melody) outline a G7 chord, and so on. This is a common type of accompaniment figure in classical music, and is referred to as "Alberti bass." Next we will look at a pop/rock comping example that uses arpeggios in the right hand.

**TRACK 10**

Pop/rock

In the first measure, the right-hand notes C-E-G-E outline a C major triad. In the second measure, the right-hand notes C-E-A-E outline an A minor triad, and so on. Notice that the right-hand arpeggios anticipate beat 3 in each measure. The left hand, meanwhile, is playing the root of each chord using a repeated eighth-note pattern. This is all typical of pop/rock comping styles.

# ARTICULATION

The *articulation* of a note describes how it is played—whether the note is short, long, accented, and so on. Applying the correct articulations to a piece of music is very important, whether it is an eighteenth-century Bach fugue, or a twenty-first-century neo-soul ballad. The following example of a D major scale shows some commonly used musical articulations.

We can analyze the above articulations as follows:

- The dot underneath the first D means *staccato* (play the note short).

- The dash underneath the E means *tenuto* (play the note long).

- The arrow underneath the F♯ is an *accent* (play the note hard).

- The arrow-with-dot underneath the G is a *staccato accent* (play the note short and hard).

- The arrow-with-dash underneath the A is a *tenuto accent* (play the note long and hard).

- The curved line connecting the B, C♯, and D is a *slur* (play *legato*, meaning smooth and connected).

# B

## BALLADS

The term *ballad* is used to describe any song played at a slow tempo. In contemporary styles, ballads typically have either an eighth-note rhythmic subdivision (as in classic pop or rock ballads, and country ballads) or a sixteenth-note rhythmic subdivision (as in modern rock and R&B ballads). Our first example is an eighth-note pop ballad pattern, using an alternating-eighth right-hand comping style.

TRACK 11

Pop ballad

This example includes several inverted chord symbols, where a major or minor triad is placed over its third or fifth in the bass. For example, the D/F# is a D major triad placed over its third (F#) in the bass, and the B/F# is a B major triad placed over its fifth (again F#) in the bass. This is a common sound in pop styles, and is often done to enable the bass line to move in a stepwise manner. The right hand is mostly using basic triads in measures 1–4, and is then embellishing with some added ninths in measures 5–8. Next we'll see the same chord progression used with a sixteenth-note R&B ballad comping pattern.

TRACK 12

R&B ballad

Here the right-hand voicings anticipate beat 3 by a sixteenth note in most measures, which is typical of R&B ballad styles. Also, the right hand is embellishing with arpeggios on beat 4 in some measures (don't overdo this!). Meanwhile, the left hand frequently anticipates beats 2 and/or 4, again normal for the style. As in the previous eighth-note ballad example, we are mostly using basic triad voicings in the first half, with some added ninths to spice things up in the second half.

In *Open Triads* (p. 86), we use this same chord progression to illustrate another very common left-hand technique for ballads.

## BASS LINES

Keyboard players are often called upon to play *bass lines*, either in the recording studio or in live performance situations. The bass part will normally be played on a synthesizer or workstation keyboard, and will use either a sample or emulation of a real bass sound, or a more electronic or synthesized bass (analog bass sounds from the Minimoog and its various clones continue to be very popular in the twenty-first century). The following examples have a synth bass part for the left hand, and an electric piano part for the right. You can play either of these parts along with the CD tracks by turning down the right or left channels.

Bass lines have the following functions (in order of importance) in contemporary styles: harmonic, rhythmic, and melodic. The first and most basic role is to define the harmony (chord progression), on the strong beats of each measure (normally beats 1 and 3 in 4/4 time), by playing the root or some other basic chord tone. The bass can also help define the rhythmic style (for example, using eighth- or sixteenth-note subdivisions, anticipations, etc.). Finally, the bass line may have an additional melodic component in more developed contemporary styles. Our first example has an eighth-note rhythmic subdivision, and is reminiscent of some of the dance/pop grooves of the 1980s.

TRACK 13

Dance/pop

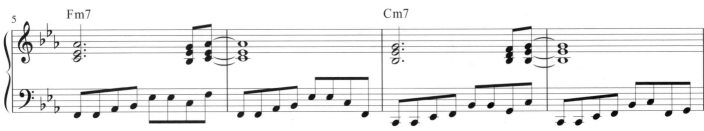

14

The bass lines on all the minor seventh chords are derived from minor pentatonic scales. The C minor pentatonic scale (containing the notes C, E♭, F, G, and B♭) is used on the Cm7 chords, and the bass line on the Fm7 and Gm7 chords uses the F and G minor pentatonic scales, respectively. The A♭ pentatonic scale (containing the notes A♭, B♭, C, E♭, and F) is used on the A♭maj7 chord. Note that the bass line always returns to the root of each chord on beat 1, while the piano voicings anticipate beat 1 of the even-numbered measures by an eighth note. This twelve-measure sequence is an example of a minor blues chord progression.

The next example applies a sixteenth-note rhythmic subdivision to the same chord progression, creating more of an R&B/funk feel.

TRACK 14

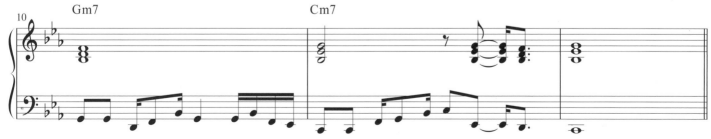

Again the bass line is substantially derived from the same pentatonic scales as in the previous example. Notice that the bass line and the piano part are "locking up" (landing at the same time) halfway through beat 3, and again on the second sixteenth note of beat 4, in all the odd-numbered measures. This is characteristic of funk styles.

### CHORD VOICING TIPS

These dance/pop and R&B/funk examples use upper-structure triads as follows:

- The Cm7, Fm7, and Gm7 chords are voiced by building major triads from the third: E♭/C, A♭/F, and B♭/G.

- The A♭maj7 chord is voiced by building a major triad from the fifth: E♭/A♭. This upgrades the chord symbol by adding the ninth (and removing the third) for a more modern sound.

Additionally, there are some embellishing triads used on the Cm7 and Fm7 chords. On the Cm7 chords, we use a B♭ major triad (built from the seventh of the Cm7 chord) between the E♭ major triads. Similarly, we use an E♭ major triad between the A♭ major triads on the Fm7 chord. Moving between two upper triads over the same chord (in this case, between major triads built from the seventh and the third of these minor seventh chords) is referred to as "alternating triads," and is a staple pop/rock harmonic technique.

# BLUES

*Blues* is an indigenous American music style that emerged in the late nineteenth century, flourished and developed in the twentieth century, and laid the foundations for modern-day R&B and rock 'n' roll styles. A number of regional blues styles have developed, including Chicago and New Orleans blues. Most blues music uses a swing-eighths rhythmic feel, and a twelve-measure progression consisting of three four-measure phrases, which start with the I, IV, and V chords of the key (chords built from the 1st, 4th, and 5th degrees), respectively. The blues does not normally use diatonic chords, instead favoring dominant chords built from these scale degrees (for example, C7, F7, and G7 chords for a blues in C). Most piano blues uses very driving and propulsive left-hand patterns, as in this Chicago blues example.

TRACK 15

Chicago blues

Note the repetitive nature of the left-hand pattern, with the root and fifth of each chord during beats 1 and 3 of each measure, and the "♭3–3" movement within beat 2. The right-hand part then plays off of this foundation, using various rhythms and syncopations.

## CHORD VOICING TIPS

This Chicago blues example uses upper-structure four-part chord shapes as follows:

- The F7 and C9 chords are voiced by building minor-seventh-flatted-fifth shapes from the third: Am7♭5/F and Em7♭5/C.

There are also various other right-hand blues devices being used as follows:

- On the C7 and G7 chords, we use 6ths (the third up to the root of the chord), embellished with a grace note a half step below the third of each chord.

- We approach measures 4 and 8 with parallel 3rds (moving by half steps), which lead into descending crossover licks.

- In measure 11, on the C7 chord, we use a repeated upper note (the root of the chord) against the moving half-step line underneath.

Next we will examine a New Orleans blues pattern. This regional blues style is somewhat different from the others in that it often uses an eight-measure form (instead of the standard twelve measures), with a straight-eighths rhythm and anticipations of beat 3, as in the following example.

TRACK 16

New Orleans blues

This time the left-hand pattern is derived from the root, third, fifth, and sixth (thirteenth) of each dominant chord.

### CHORD VOICING TIPS

This New Orleans blues uses some upper-triad movement on each chord: the B♭-F major triad movement on the F7 chord, the E♭-B♭ major triad movement on the B♭7 chord, and so on. This type of IV-I triad movement is known as "backcycling," and is a staple sound in blues, gospel, and rock styles.

### FURTHER READING

For more info on blues piano, please check out my *Blues Piano: The Complete Guide with CD!*, published by Hal Leonard Corporation.

# BLUES SCALE

The *blues scale* is a six-note scale that is widely used in blues, rock, R&B, funk, and gospel styles. Here is a C blues scale.

TRACK 17
Part 1

The C blues scale contains the following notes (with intervals above the tonic C in parentheses): C, E♭ (minor 3rd), F (perfect 4th), F♯ (augmented 4th), G (perfect 5th), and B♭ (minor 7th). This scale is equivalent to the C minor pentatonic scale, with an added F♯.

The following example shows a blues melody over a twelve-measure blues progression in C. The melody breaks down into three similar four-measure phrases, each starting on an upbeat, which is very typical of blues phrasing. The entire C blues scale shown above is used over the C7, F7, and G7 chords. You can probably hear that some of these notes sound tense over these chords; we get away with this because of the unique melodic character of the blues scale—in fact, these tensions are one of the defining characteristics of the blues.

TRACK 17
Part 2

Basic shuffle blues

Note that the left-hand pattern is alternating between the root-plus-fifth and root-plus-sixth of each chord. This pattern sounds great on many blues and blues/rock songs, and works within both swing-eighths and straight-eighths rhythmic feels.

# BOOGIE-WOOGIE

*Boogie-woogie* styles emerged in the early part of the twentieth century, and featured fast tempos and driving left-hand patterns. Both the left and right hands often play single-note lines, as opposed to the more chord-based patterns used in later blues styles. The eighth notes are almost always swung. This example features a classic boogie-woogie left-hand pattern, using octaves to outline the notes in each chord.

TRACK 18

Boogie-woogie

The left-hand octaves outline the root, third, fifth, sixth (thirteenth), and seventh of the chords in measures 1–8, and just the root, third, and fifth of the chords in measures 9–11 (with the sixth added in measure 10). Meanwhile, the right hand is playing melodic runs using half steps and whole steps: the E-F-F♯-G run (connecting the third to the fifth on the C7 chord), the E♭-F-F♯-G run (connecting the seventh to the ninth on the F7 chord), and so on. The right hand also leads into some basic chord tones with grace notes a half step below: into the third of C7, and into the sevenths of F7 and G7. We're also using some 6ths: from the C Mixolydian mode in measure 4, approaching the fifth and seventh of the C7 chord by half step in measures 2 and 8, and approaching the third and fifth of the F7 chord by half step in measure 6.

## CHORD VOICING TIPS

This boogie-woogie example uses upper-structure four-part chord shapes as follows:

- The D♭9 and C9 chords are voiced by building minor-seventh-flatted-fifth shapes from the third: Fm7♭5/D♭ and Em7♭5/C.

## CHART

A *chart* is a notated version of a song, showing the melody and chord symbols, or just the chord symbols without the melody. A chart should also show the overall form and sections of the song (intro, verse, chorus, etc.), as well as any road map instructions, which can include repeats of sections, D.C. (meaning go back to the beginning), D.S. (meaning go back to the "sign"), when to go to the coda (end section), and so on.

If the chart has melody and chord symbols, it is also referred to as a lead sheet. If a chart just has chord symbols, it is also referred to as a *chord chart*. A fake book is a collection of lead sheets, normally in a particular style (i.e., pop/rock, jazz standards, etc.). Chord charts are not normally found in books, but are prepared by musicians and bands as needed for rehearsal or performance. When presented with a chord chart or lead sheet, the musician needs to improvise the part, based on an understanding of the style. See *Faking It* (p. 43).

A chord chart might just consist of chord symbols and slashes. This tells the musician to comp (accompany) according to the style, as in the following example.

Sometimes the chord chart might include rhythmic information (in which case the slashes are given precise rhythmic values), with the specific voicings still being left up to the player.

A lead sheet, then, will include the melody as well as the chord symbols.

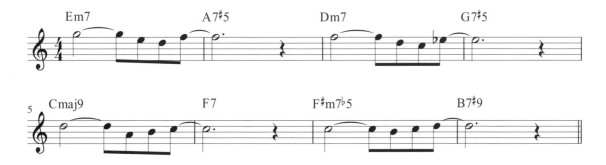

Many experienced keyboardists prefer to see a lead sheet rather than a chord chart even when accompanying (especially in jazz styles), to help ensure that the part they play is complementary to and supportive of the melody.

## CHORD INVERSIONS

All triads and seventh chords can be *inverted* (i.e., re-arranged so that the root is no longer on the bottom). This may be done for several reasons, including:

- To voice lead smoothly between chords, avoiding unnecessary skips;

- To place a desired melody note on top of a chord;

- To accommodate a desired register or range for a particular keyboard sound, or to combine better with other instruments.

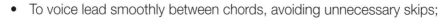

TRACK 19  Any triad can be inverted, as shown in the following examples.
Part 1

**Triad inversions**

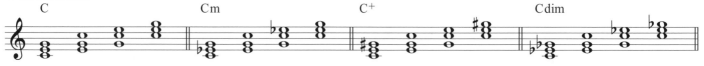

We can analyze the C major triads in the first measure as follows:

- The first triad is in root position, with the root on the bottom.

- The second triad is in first inversion, with the third on the bottom.

- The third triad is in second inversion, with the fifth on the bottom.

- The last triad is again in root position, an octave higher than the first.

Similar logic and terminology applies to minor, augmented, and diminished triads.

Any seventh chord can also be inverted. The following example shows inversions of three
TRACK 19  types of seventh chord (major seventh, minor seventh, and dominant seventh).
Part 2

**Seventh chord inversions**

We can analyze the C major seventh chords in the first measure as follows:

- The first chord is in root position, with the root on the bottom.

- The second chord is in first inversion, with the third on the bottom.

- The third chord is in second inversion, with the fifth on the bottom.

- The fourth chord is in third inversion, with the seventh on the bottom.

Similar logic and terminology applies to the minor seventh and dominant seventh chords.

# CHORD PROGRESSIONS

A *chord progression* is the sequence of chords used in a song. If the player is reading from a chart, the chord progression is normally the minimum level of information required, together with the form and road map of the song.

Being able to spell the chords in a given progression is, of course, important, but it is only the first step to interpreting and performing a song at a professional level. More experienced players will have different voicing choices to interpret chord symbols and progressions, as well as rhythmic patterns appropriate to the style.

Subject to many variations, there are three broad categories of chord progressions used in today's music.

   **1) Diatonic:** all chords contained within a key.

2) **Chromatic unaltered**: chords borrowed from other keys, but still not altered (i.e., no sharped or flatted fifths and/or ninths).

3) **Chromatic altered**: chords borrowed from other keys, and with sharped or flatted fifths and/or ninths; normally indicative of jazz styles.

Another important variable is the size of the chords used: simpler pop styles favor triad progressions, whereas four-part (and larger) chords are normally found in R&B and jazz-influenced styles. Here are some examples of these different categories of chord progression.

In this progression of simple triads, all the chords are diatonic to (contained within) the key of G. This is typical of a simple pop ballad or rock song.

In this progression, all the chords are major sevenths, and they move between different keys. This is typical of more advanced rock or R&B styles.

This more sophisticated progression uses altered dominant chords in different keys, typical of jazz and Latin styles.

## FURTHER READING

For more information on the different types of chord progressions used in pop, rock, and jazz styles, please check out my *Contemporary Music Theory: Level Two*, published by Hal Leonard Corporation.

# CHORD SYMBOL

A *chord symbol* is a symbol placed above the staff, telling you which chord is being used at that point in the music. Chord symbols normally have two components.

- A root note, telling you what the root of the chord is
- A suffix, telling you the type of chord

For example, the chord symbol "Cmaj7" has a root note of "C" and a suffix of "maj7," which tells you this is a C major seventh chord. If a chord symbol consists of only a root note with no suffix, then the chord is a major triad (for example, the chord symbol "C" signifies a C major triad).

When looking at a chord symbol, more experienced players will know what overall chord type it indicates (major, minor, dominant, diminished, etc.) For example, C, Cmaj7, Cmaj9, and C(add9) are all chords of the major type. Recognizing this helps with voicing choices, and in understanding the function of the chord within the progression.

The chord symbols that you see on charts will normally fall into one of the following categories.

- Triads: i.e., C, Cm, Caug, Cdim

- Seventh chords: i.e., Cmaj7, Cm7, C7

- Add9 chords, which add the 9th but exclude the 7th: i.e., C(add9), Am(add9)

- Ninth chords: i.e., the Dmaj9 and B♭maj9 chords used on **Track 7** (p. 9)

- Eleventh chords: i.e., the Dm11 chords used on **Track 71** (p. 97)

- Thirteenth chords: i.e., the A13 chord used on **Track 45** (p. 62)

- "Slash" chord symbols, most often used to indicate an inverted chord (a chord with a tone other than the root in the bass): i.e., the Em/G and B/F♯ chords used on **Tracks 11** and **12** (p. 13)

- Suspended chords, which replace the third with another note—either the fourth/eleventh (sus4) or the second/ninth (sus2): i.e., the sus4 chords on **Track 78, part 1** (p. 107).

- Altered chords, which flat or sharp the fifth and/or ninth of the chord: i.e., the D7(♯5,♭9) and D7(♯5,♯9) chords used on **Track 8** (p. 10).

Unfortunately, the world of chord symbols is rather "unregulated," meaning that the same chord may be indicated with several different chord symbols. For instance, this book uses the symbol "Cm7" for a C minor seventh chord, but you may also see this written as "Cmi7," "Cmin7," or "C-7."

### FURTHER READING

This page is only a brief summary of a rather large subject! For much more information on all chord types and functions, commonly used chord symbols, scale sources, and all possible chord extensions and alterations, please check out my *Contemporary Music Theory: Level Three*, published by Hal Leonard Corporation.

## COMPING

*Comping* is a musical slang term for accompaniment. At a professional level, musicians will comp through a song based on their understanding of harmony and style. In other words, they will create stylistically appropriate voicings from the chord symbols, and then play them using a suitable rhythmic pattern. We will now take a couple of chord charts and comp on them in different styles.

Jazz swing – chord chart

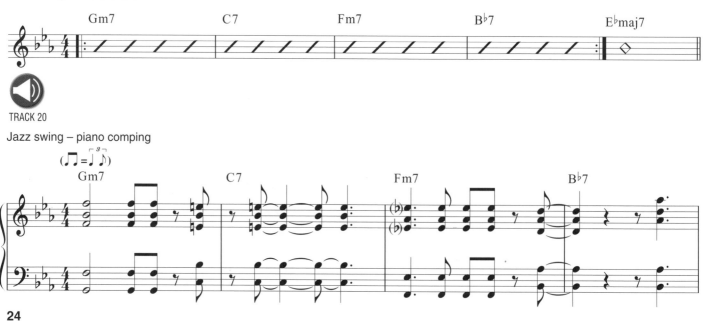

TRACK 20

Jazz swing – piano comping

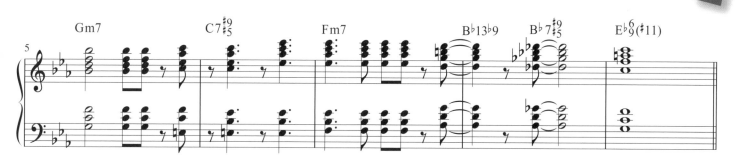

In the first four measures of the comping solution, the piano part is using "7–3" voicings (the seventh and third of each chord) in the right hand, over root-seventh intervals in the left hand. This is a staple jazz voicing technique, used here with rhythmic anticipations typical of swing styles. In the last five measures, we switch to polychord (chord-over-chord) voicings, with the left hand playing double-4th shapes (three notes stacked as two 4ths) under right-hand triads. This modern voicing style was pioneered by jazz piano icons Bill Evans and McCoy Tyner. Note that this upgrades the chords with extensions and alterations (which are reflected in the revised chord symbols). This kind of chord upgrading is routine in jazz styles.

## CHORD VOICING TIPS

In measures 5–9, this example uses double 4ths in the left hand and triads in the right hand as follows:

- The Gm7 and Fm7 chords are voiced by building major triads from the third in the right hand, over a double-4th shape (root-eleventh-seventh) built from the root in the left hand.

- The C7(#5,#9) chord is voiced by building a major triad from the sharped fifth in the right hand, over a double-4th shape (third-seventh-sharped ninth) built from the third in the left hand.

- The B♭13♭9 chord is voiced by building a major triad from the thirteenth in the right hand, over a double-4th shape (seventh-third-thirteenth) built from the seventh in the left hand.

- The B♭7(#5,#9) chord is voiced by building a major triad from the sharped fifth in the right hand, over a double-4th shape (seventh-third-sharped fifth) built from the seventh in the left hand.

- The E♭6/9(#11) chord is voiced by building a major triad from the ninth in the right hand, over a double-4th shape (third-sixth-ninth) built from the third in the left hand.

Blues/rock – chord chart

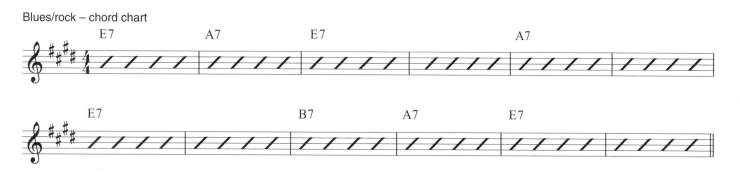

TRACK 21

Blues/rock – piano comping

This blues/rock comping solution uses 3rds from different Mixolydian modes. The scale source for an E7 chord is the E Mixolydian mode (E-F#-G#-A-B-C#-D); if you look in the first measure on the E7 chord, the right-hand intervals G#-B, A-C#, and B-D come from this mode. Similarly, in measure 5 the right hand intervals C#-E, D-F#, and E-G come from the A Mixolydian mode, and so on. Note that the top notes of these intervals are the fifth, sixth (thirteenth), and seventh of each dominant chord—these top notes are commonly used with the Mixolydian intervals. Grace notes approaching the third and/or fifth of a chord have also been used—another staple blues piano technique. Meanwhile, the left hand is playing a basic root-fifth and root-sixth pattern on each chord, giving solid support to the right-hand voicings.

## FURTHER READING

For more info on the double-4th shapes and polychords used in the jazz swing example, please check out my book *Contemporary Music Theory: Level Three*. And for more on blues and blues/rock styles, see my *Blues Piano: The Complete Guide with CD!* Both books are published by Hal Leonard Corporation.

# COUNTRY

*Country* is an American music style that emerged in the 1920s, and continues to evolve into the twenty-first century. Traditional country music uses basic chord progressions (i.e., I-IV-V), swing-eighths rhythms, and simple song forms. More modern country styles frequently borrow from pop and rock music, using straight-eighths rhythms and more sophisticated harmonies. Our first example is in a traditional country style, using a I-IV-V triad progression in the key of G.

TRACK 22

The right hand is playing basic triads derived from the chord symbols, and is using alternating eighths with rests on beats 1 and 3, which is typical of basic country comping. Walkups and walkdowns are being used to connect chords with roots a 4th apart; for example, there is a walkup in measure 2 (from the G chord up to the C chord), and a walkdown in measure 4 (from the C chord back down to the G chord). Walkups and walkdowns normally have three different components:

- A bass line that walks up the scale (i.e., the left-hand G-G-A-B in measure 2, leading to C in the next measure)

- A line moving a 10th (octave plus a 3rd) above the bass line (i.e., the right-hand B-C-D in measure 2)

- A drone (repeated note) above the line moving in 10ths with the bass (i.e., the repeated G in measure 2 in the right hand)—the drone note is normally the root of the chord when walking up, and the fifth of the chord when walking down.

Elsewhere, the left hand is playing the root of the chord on beat 1, and the fifth of the chord on beat 3. Next we'll look at a more modern country/rock example.

Country/rock

This time the right-hand part is based on pentatonic scales built from the root of each chord. For example, in measure 1 on the A major chord we are using the A pentatonic scale (A, B, C#, E, F#). The note E (the fifth of the chord) is being used as a drone, and below the drone we are alternating (sometimes referred to as "hammering") between B and C# (the next two notes below in the pentatonic scale) using grace notes. The intervals between these notes and the drone note create that characteristic country sound. The drone note is normally either the root or fifth of the chord, and sometimes both of these may be used within a phrase (for example, both A and E are used as drones in measure 15 on the A major chord).

On the A major chords in measures 2 and 10, we move between the 3rds D-F# and C#-E, implying a D major-to-A major triad movement. This type of IV-I triad movement within a chord is called "backcycling," and is used across a range of contemporary styles. Similar movements occur on the G major chords, and on the E major chord in measure 14 (here with the 3rds inverted to become 6ths).

### FURTHER READING

For more information on country and country/rock styles, please check out my *Country Piano: The Complete Guide with CD!*, published by Hal Leonard Corporation.

# CROSSOVER LICKS

*Crossover licks* or phrases are an indispensable part of the blues piano vocabulary. They are descending right-hand phrases (normally including arpeggios) that require the upper fingers of the right hand to cross over the thumb on the way to the lower notes in the phrase. These are also sometimes referred to as "resolving" licks, as they normally end with a half-step resolution into the third of the chord. All of the following examples work over a C or C7 chord. You should learn them in as many keys as possible—they come in really handy!

TRACK 24

## DIATONIC SEVENTH CHORDS

The word "diatonic" means "belonging to a major scale or key"; therefore, *diatonic seventh chords* are all found within the key being used. Simpler contemporary styles often stay within the restriction of a single key, and in this case the two most common sources of chords are diatonic triads and diatonic seventh chords. Compared to diatonic triads, these four-part chords are fuller and sound a little more sophisticated. Here are the commonly used diatonic seventh chords in the key of C major.

Next we will use these chords in a simple R&B ballad setting.

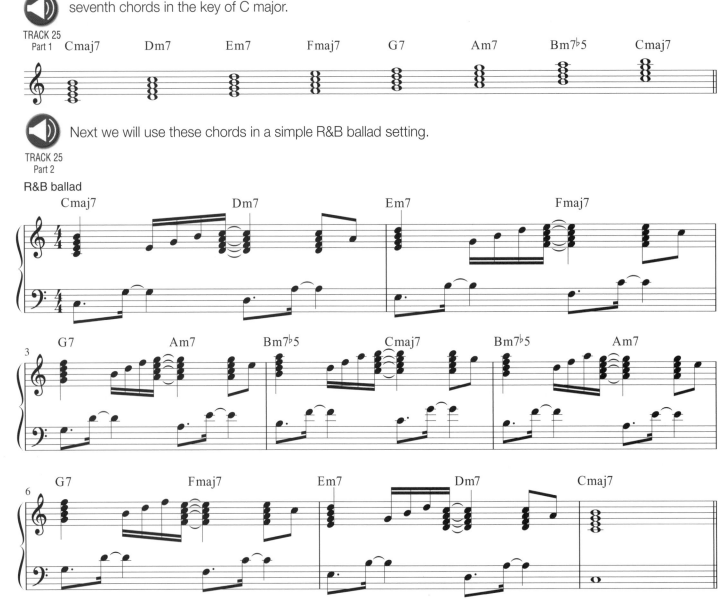

This example uses the chords in root position, though they can, of course, be inverted. Normal R&B ballad rhythmic stylings are being used: the right hand is anticipating beat 3 of each measure by a sixteenth note (and arpeggiating the chord during beat 2), and the left hand is playing a root-fifth pattern on each chord, landing on beats 1 and 3 and anticipating beats 2 and 4.

### FURTHER READING

For more information on diatonic seventh chords, please check out my *Contemporary Music Theory: Level One*, published by Hal Leonard Corporation.

# DIATONIC TRIADS

The word "diatonic" means "belonging to a major scale or key"; therefore, *diatonic triads* are all found within the key being used. Simpler contemporary styles often stay within the restriction of a single key, and in this case the two most common sources of chords are diatonic seventh chords and diatonic triads. Compared to diatonic seventh chords, these three-note chords are less dense and sound more basic. Here are the diatonic triads in the key of C major.

TRACK 26
Part 1

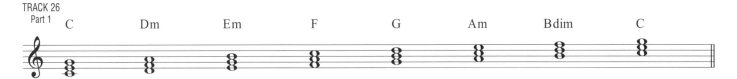

Next we will use these triads in a simple pop/rock setting.

TRACK 26
Part 2

This example uses the chords in root position, though they can, of course, be inverted as needed. Normal pop/rock rhythmic stylings are being used: the right hand is playing a two-measure rhythmic phrase with eighth-note anticipations and the left hand is playing the root of each chord in octaves, with the lowest note on beats 1 and 3 and the highest note on beats 2 and 4 (with eighth-note pickups leading into beat 3).

## FURTHER READING

For more information on diatonic triads, please check out my *Contemporary Music Theory: Level One*, published by Hal Leonard Corporation.

# DIGITAL AUDIO WORKSTATION

A *digital audio workstation* (DAW) is a piece of software running on a Mac and/or Windows PC platform that enables you to record, edit, and produce music. Many of these started out as MIDI sequencers some years ago, and then added audio recording facilities as computer processing power increased. Leading examples of workstation software in 2007 (with manufacturers in parentheses) are:

| | |
|---|---|
| **Mac only**: | Digital Performer (Mark of the Unicorn) |
| | Logic (Apple) |
| **PC only**: | Sonar (Cakewalk) |
| | Acid (Sony) |
| **Mac and PC**: | Pro Tools (Digidesign) |
| | Cubase (Steinberg) |
| | Live (Ableton) |
| | Tracktion (Mackie) |

When recording using one of these products, there are two basic ways to access sounds:

1) **Using MIDI keyboards and/or sound modules**.

   This is mature technology that has been around since the 1980s, and is still used today. MIDI stands for "musical instrument digital interface," and is a protocol by which keyboards, computers, and other pieces of equipment communicate with each other. You hook up your MIDI keyboard to the computer (normally via a MIDI interface), hit "record" on your workstation software, and then play your keyboard. The music is recorded as MIDI data in the computer. When you have the computer play it back, the MIDI data is re-directed out to your keyboard (or to any other MIDI device in your setup) so that you can hear what you recorded. You can then repeat this process for the other tracks on your song, and so forth.

2) **Using plug-in software**.

   This has been in common use since the late 1990s, with the advent of faster and more powerful computers. Instead of directing MIDI data to an external device, the MIDI data can trigger a synthesizer or sound library from within the computer itself (via a plug-in piece of software, which works within the host workstation software). The computer is then connected to an audio interface to convert the data back into an audio signal so that you can hear it. Plug-in technology is of particular interest to piano players, who use plug-ins such as Ivory (manufactured by Synthogy) to play and record acoustic piano sounds with an uncanny degree of realism. Software workstations also record audio data alongside MIDI data, and the audio interface is again used for the purpose of converting the audio (vocal, saxophone, etc.) into digital data for the software to record.

Compared to stand-alone workstation keyboards and personal digital studio hardware devices, the pros and cons of digital audio workstation software are:

**Pros**: High-quality sounds and extensive editing facilities (and getting better all the time), with the number of tracks and simultaneous sounds limited only by your computer power. This is the best and most flexible way to record music at home, if you have the budget.

**Cons**: More expensive than stand-alone systems. Steeper learning curve involved.

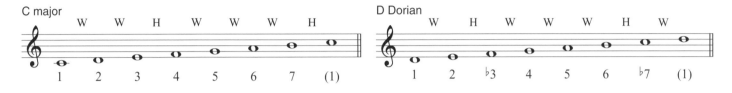

# DORIAN MODE

A mode (or modal scale) is created when we take a major scale and displace it to start on another scale degree. An example of this is the *Dorian mode*, created when the major scale is displaced to start on the 2nd degree. The following example shows a C major scale displaced to create a D Dorian mode.

If you compare these two scales, you'll see that the notes are the same; they just begin and end in a different place. Thus, each has a different tonic and a different pattern of whole and half steps. You can also think of the Dorian mode as a major scale with flatted 3rd and 7th degrees (1-2-♭3-4-5-6-♭7). This mode has a minor sound and is a basic scale source for a minor seventh chord. We could say that C major is the relative major scale of D Dorian, as C major was the scale originally displaced to create the mode.

To use a Dorian mode harmonically, we would simply put the tonic of the mode (D in the above example) in the bass, and then place notes and/or chords from the mode (or from its relative major) above this bass note. A common tactic is to use diatonic triads from the relative major. For example, the diatonic triads in C major are C, Dm, Em, F, G, Am, and Bdim. Placing any of these—particularly IV and V (i.e., F and G)—above the tonic D is an effective way to create Dorian harmony.

Our first example is in the '60s cool-jazz style of Miles Davis and Wynton Kelly, and uses the E and F Dorian modes. When using E Dorian (measures 1–8 and 13–14), we play G and A triads in the right hand, which are IV and V of the relative major scale (D major). These triads can also be thought of as ♭III and IV with respect to the root of the implied Em7 chord. Similarly, when using F Dorian in measures 9–12, we use A♭ and B♭ triads in the right hand.

TRACK 27

This is a typical modal jazz example from the period, with the left hand outlining the roots, fifths, and sevenths of the Em7 and Fm7 chords (and staying within the E and F Dorian modes, respectively).

Next up we have a '70s-style jazz/funk groove using Dorian modes and triads.

TRACK 28

Jazz/funk

This example uses the C Dorian mode in measures 1–4 and 7–9, with E♭ and F triads in the right-hand part (IV and V of B♭ major, the relative major scale of C Dorian). Similarly, when using E♭ Dorian in measures 5–6, we have G♭ and A♭ triads in the right hand (from the D♭ major scale). Note the sixteenth-note anticipations, and the rhythmic conversation between the right- and left-hand parts—all very typical of funk keyboard styles.

Also notice that both of these Dorian examples use a lot of inverted triads in the right-hand parts. Modal triads tend to sound better when inverted. Second-inversion triads are used the most, due to their strong and powerful sound.

For another important mode, see *Mixolydian Mode* (p. 76).

## DOTTED NOTES

Whenever a dot is placed after a note, it adds half as much again to the rhythmic value or length (in other words, it multiplies the existing length by 1.5), as in the following example.

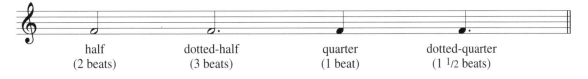

| half | dotted-half | quarter | dotted-quarter |
|------|-------------|---------|----------------|
| (2 beats) | (3 beats) | (1 beat) | (1 $\frac{1}{2}$ beats) |

Without the dot, the second note above would just be a half note (lasting for 2 beats). But with the dot added, we add half as much again to the original length, so the note now lasts for 3 beats. Likewise, without the dot the fourth note would just be a quarter note (lasting for 1 beat). But the dot adds half as much again to the original length, so the note now lasts for 1½ beats.

Next we will see some ways in which these dotted notes can be used in a melody. If we use a dotted half note (3 beats) together with a quarter note (1 beat), the resulting total of four beats will fill a 4/4 measure. If we use a dotted quarter note (1 ½ beats) together with an eighth note (1/2 beat), the resulting total of two beats could occupy the first or second half of a 4/4 measure. These are very common rhythmic combinations, as shown in this melody example.

1 & 2 & 3 & 4 &    1 & 2 & 3 & 4 &    1 & 2 & 3 & 4 &    1 & 2 & 3 & 4 &

Notice the eighth-note counting (1 & 2 & 3 & 4 &, etc.) in this example. It's good to be able to count through rhythmic figures in this way when necessary. Although experienced readers will recognize most rhythms at sight, they'll still need to count out rhythms once in a while!

## DOWNBEATS

A *downbeat* falls on the beat (i.e., on beat 1, 2, 3, or 4 in a 4/4 measure)—as opposed to an *upbeat*, which falls in between the beats. This is illustrated as follows:

1       &       2       &       3       &       4       &

When we count eighth-note rhythms this way (1 & 2 &, etc.), we can see that the downbeats fall on 1, 2, 3, and 4, and the upbeats fall on the &s in between (referred to as the "and" of 1, "and" of 2, etc.).

Basic rock styles often emphasize downbeats, as in the following example:

In case you haven't seen it before... a chord symbol with a "5" suffix means "root and fifth only" (equivalent to a triad with the third omitted). This is a common sound in hard rock and metal styles.

## CHORD VOICING TIPS

This hard rock example mostly uses open root-fifth-root or fifth-root-fifth voicings in the right hand, with some variations as follows:

- The Esus4 chords are voiced as fourth-root-fourth (the fourth, A, being the suspension).

- The D(add9) and C(add9) chords are voiced as fifth-ninth-fifth (a very useful modern rock sound).

Also, the single eighth notes on the "and" of 2 and the "and" of 4 are adding the following chord extensions:

- The ninth of the chords in measures 1–2 and 5–6.

- The suspended fourth/eleventh of the chords in measures 3, 7, and 9.

# EAR TRAINING

*Ear training* is a vital area of your musicianship, particularly if you are playing contemporary styles such as pop, rock, and jazz. Ear training has two very important benefits for today's piano players:

1)  It helps you hear ahead in your playing and writing.

2)  It helps you recognize and transcribe music that you hear.

My ear training books and classes use the solfège system.

In this case DO (the tonic, or home base) is the note C; however DO could be assigned to any note (this is sometimes referred to as a moveable-DO concept).

The first step in our ear training is to recognize the movements between active tones and resting tones in the major scale. We hear these movements in relation to DO, the tonic of the scale.

TRACK 30

In all major keys, the following active tones like to move (or resolve) to their resting neighbors:

• The 2nd degree (RE) resolves down to the 1st degree (DO).

• The 4th degree (FA) resolves down to the 3rd degree (MI).

• The 6th degree (LA) resolves down to the 5th degree (SO).

• The 7th degree (TI) resolves up to the 1st degree (DO).

Simpler melodies (for example, folk and traditional songs) normally contain a lot of these resolutions. More sophisticated styles will not always resolve the active tones to their adjacent resting tones; however, an active tone will still sound active, whether or not the resolution to the adjacent resting tone actually occurs. Here is a vocal exercise that you can use to begin recognizing these resolutions in the major scale.

TRACK 31

When you can recognize these sounds by ear, you'll have completed an important first step in your ear training!

**FURTHER READING**

Ear training is a big subject, which I have written complete courses on! Please check out my *Contemporary Eartraining: Levels One* and *Two*, both published by Hal Leonard Corporation.

# EIGHTH NOTES AND RESTS

An *eighth note* lasts for a half a beat. This is also equivalent to an eighth of a measure in 4/4 time. Here is an example of some different ways that eighth notes can be written.

The rhythmic counting (1 & 2 & 3 & 4 &, etc.) is shown below the notes in this measure.

An eighth note is written with a black (or filled-in) notehead, with a stem attached, and either a flag if the note is by itself (like the first four notes in the above example) or a beam if the note is joined to other notes (as in the remaining notes in the example). Sometimes the beam may join two eighth notes together within one beat (as in the second half of the first measure), or the beam may join all of the eighth notes within two successive beats (as in the second measure).

Next we'll see an example of an eighth rest (which also lasts for half a beat).

Here's a notation example that combines eighth notes and rests.

In the above example, the eighth rests fall on beats 3 and 4 in measures 1 and 3. Note that the rhythmic sum of all the notes and rests in each measure agrees with the time signature (i.e., four beats for each 4/4 measure).

For information on other basic rhythmic values, see *Half Notes and Rests* (p. 56), *Quarter Notes and Rests* (p. 95), *Sixteenth Notes and Rests* (p. 104), and *Whole Notes and Rests* (p. 121).

# EIGHT-NOTE SCALES

*Eight-note* (or *octatonic*) *scales* are the result of dividing an octave into four equal parts, and then further subdividing into half steps and whole steps. For example, if we take an octave from middle C up to the C an octave higher, and divide it into four equal parts, we get C-E♭-F♯-A-C (which actually spells a C diminished seventh chord). Each of the internal intervals is a minor 3rd (three half steps). If we then further divide each of these minor 3rds into a half-step/whole-step pair, we get an eight-note dominant scale.

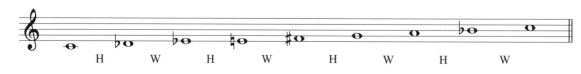

As this scale starts with a half step, and alternates between half steps and whole steps throughout, it is sometimes referred to as a "half-step/whole-step scale." The name "dominant scale" is applied because the scale can be used over a dominant chord.

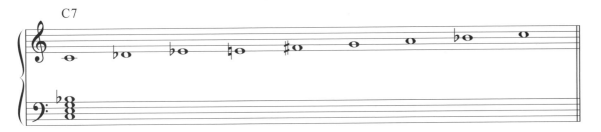

In addition to the basic chord tones of the C7 chord, this scale also adds the following extensions and alterations: ♭9, ♯9, ♯11, and 13.

Alternatively, if we divide each internal minor 3rd (C-E♭-F♯-A-C) into a whole-step/half-step pair (instead of half-step/whole-step), we get an eight-note diminished scale.

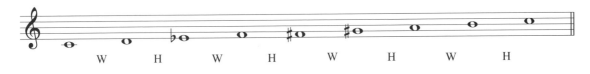

As this scale starts with a whole step, and alternates between whole steps and half steps throughout, it is sometimes referred to as a "whole-step/half-step scale." The name "diminished scale" is applied because the scale can be used over a diminished chord.

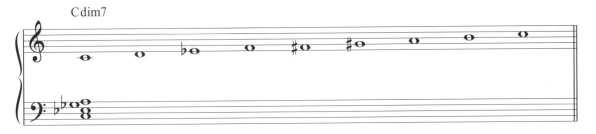

In addition to the basic chord tones of the Cdim7 chord, this scale also adds the following extensions and alterations: 9, 11, ♭13, and 14 (a major 7th above the root).

### FURTHER READING

For more information on eight-note scales and their uses over different chords, please check out my *Contemporary Music Theory: Level Three*, published by Hal Leonard Corporation.

# EQUIPMENT

*Equipment* is a big topic for today's musician! In this brief summary, we'll discuss acoustic pianos and electronic pianos/keyboards—which will hopefully help when you make your next equipment purchase.

When you strike a key on an acoustic piano, a felt-covered hammer strikes the strings to produce the sound—a purely physical process. By contrast, when you strike a key on an electronic keyboard, the sound is generated digitally, and the signal needs to be fed to an amplifier and speakers (either in the instrument itself, or a separate system) in order for it to be heard.

Here is a quick summary of the pros and cons of acoustic and electronic instruments.

### Acoustic

**Pros**: Unique sound (the "real thing"), with physical responsiveness and sensitivity that are not easy to duplicate with electronic instruments.

**Cons**: Higher cost; more maintenance required; take up more space; harder to move; harder to record.

### Electronic

**Pros**: Lower cost; less maintenance required; smaller footprint; better portability; easier to record. Continually better approximations of that distinctive piano sound (the "real thing").

**Cons**: Keyboard often lacks the weight, responsiveness, and sensitivity of the real piano. Needs electricity and a speaker system.

There are two fundamental categories of acoustic pianos: vertical (upright) and horizontal (grand). Grand pianos have a louder and fuller tone than uprights, due to their longer strings and larger soundboards. However, upright pianos are less expensive and have a considerably smaller footprint.

Studio piano

Baby grand piano

There are three basic categories of electronic pianos and keyboard instruments (with many hybrids and variations): digital pianos, synthesizers and workstations, and software instruments.

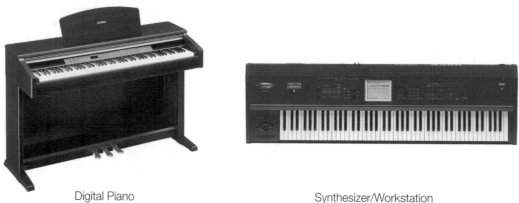
Digital Piano

Synthesizer/Workstation

1) **Digital pianos** are often the most tempting option for people who want a sound close to the "real thing," and who don't want to deal with computers and MIDI technology. They have eighty-eight weighted keys, and come with a selection of piano sounds as well as a handful of other sounds. They are designed to be used as stand-alone instruments, either in the home or in a school classroom. They normally have built-in speakers, and a headphone output so you can practice quietly.

2) **Synthesizers and workstations** constitute a vast category! Synthesizers are keyboard instruments capable of playing different sounds, which by the late 1980s typically included samples (digital recordings) of real instruments, including piano. When onboard sequencing (multi-channel recording) was added to these keyboards, workstations were born. Functionally today's workstations are similar, but with more features, memory, sounds, and polyphony (number of voices that can sound at once). These instruments normally don't have built-in speakers, so you need to run them through an external amplifier and speaker system (or combo amp) or listen to them on headphones.

3) **Software instruments** offer the greatest realism if you need to get as close as possible to the real sound of a piano. These instruments can run on a Mac or PC, or can be installed in a rack-mount computer device such as the Muse Receptor. You then hook up your MIDI controller (a keyboard capable of generating MIDI data, which almost all modern keyboards do) to the computer or rack device. You may also need an audio interface to convert the digital signal back into audio, so as to feed it to your speaker system. Software instruments take advantage of the faster speed of today's computers (together with large hard drives and fast access times) to store huge sample libraries of instrument sounds, far larger than the memory available on workstation synths. For piano sounds, this means individual samples of multiple velocity levels per note, which all adds up to an unprecedented level of realism. You've already heard software pianos on many recordings (though you may not have realized that it wasn't the "real thing")!

# EXERCISES

This section contains some *exercises* to use for warm-up purposes, and to help build your piano technique. First we'll look at an arpeggio exercise.

TRACK 32

Major-triad arpeggio exercise

Try to articulate this exercise as evenly and cleanly as you can. Note that the first four measures outline a C major triad, and the next four measures outline a D♭ major triad. You should then continue these arpeggios in an ascending chromatic sequence (i.e., D, E♭, E♮, F, and so on). This is a great warm-up, and will also come in handy in various contemporary styles.

**E**

Next up is a pentatonic scale exercise.

TRACK 33

Pentatonic scale exercise

Note that the first eight measures use a C pentatonic scale, and the next eight measures use a D♭ pentatonic scale. You should then continue the exercise in an ascending chromatic sequence (i.e., D, E♭, E♮, F, and so on). This exercise uses pentatonic-scale subgroups (contiguous groups of notes within the scale). For example, in measure 1 we start off with C-D-E-G in both hands, followed by D-E-G-A, E-G-A-C, and so on. Having these subgroups under your fingers is also very useful when improvising in contemporary styles. For example, see the country/rock improvisation in *Soloing* (p. 105).

To develop your technical facility further, check out the Hanon exercises (*The Virtuoso Pianist* by Charles Louis Hanon), available from most music stores. These are excellent for developing finger independence, and are also great for warm-ups.

# FAKING IT

A musician is *faking it* when he or she improvises a comping (accompaniment) or melody treatment of a song, working either from a chart or from memory. This requires an ability to voice chords in a stylistically appropriate manner, and a knowledge of the various rhythmic patterns used for each style. Here's a comping example in a pop/rock style.

Pop/rock: chord chart

TRACK 34

Pop/rock comping

In measures 1–8, the right hand is playing upper-structure triads, and the left hand is providing a steady eighth-note pulse, playing the root of each chord. In measures 9–16, the right hand switches to a series of 4ths, over a left-hand octave pattern on the root of each chord.

## CHORD VOICING TIPS

In measures 1–8, this pop/rock example uses alternating triads in the right hand, similar to those on **Track 14** (p. 15).

- Alternating between major triads built from the seventh and the third, on both the Dm7 and Gm7 chords.

- Alternating between major triads built from the fourth and the root, on the C chord. This interior IV-I triad movement is also known as "backcycling," which is also used on **Track 16** (p. 17).

In measures 9–16, this example uses 4ths derived from the D minor pentatonic scale (equivalent to the F pentatonic scale) in the right hand. These intervals (G-C, A-D, C-F, and D-G) float over the different chords, which works because the whole progression is in the key of D minor. This is a signature rock music sound.

Next we'll look at a leadsheet that has melody and chord symbols. This time we need to play the melody, not just comp over the changes.

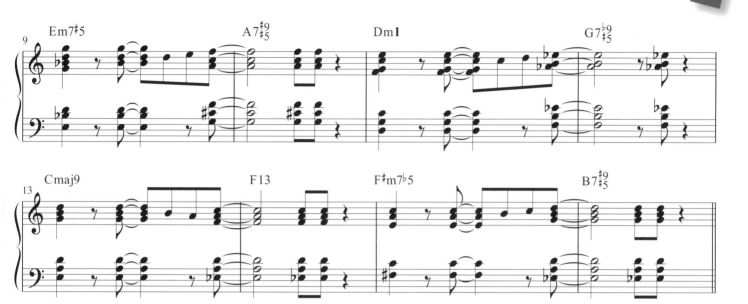

This jazz swing example uses "7-3" voicings (the sevenths and thirds of the chords) below the melody in measures 1–8. As we saw when comping on the first half of **Track 20** (p. 24), these voicings are a good solution in mainstream jazz styles. In this melody treatment, the upper fingers of the right hand are playing the melody, and the lower fingers of the right hand are playing the "7-3" voicings in between the melody, using typical jazz swing rhythmic figures and syncopation. The left hand is playing root-seventh intervals, with the root on beat 1 or anticipating beat 1, and the seventh "locking up" with the right-hand voicings. In measures 9–16, we switch to polychord voicings, with the left hand playing double-4th shapes (a stack of two 4ths) and the right hand playing triads. This is similar to the second half of **Track 20** (p. 25), now with the right-hand triads inverted to place the melody notes on top.

## CHORD VOICING TIPS

In measures 9–16, this jazz swing example uses double 4ths in the left hand, and triads in the right hand, as follows:

- The Em7♭5 and F♯m7♭5 chords are voiced by building minor triads from the third in the right hand, over a double-4th shape (root-flatted fifth-seventh) or a root-flatted fifth interval built from the root in the left hand.

- The Dm11 chord is voiced by building a major triad from the seventh in the right hand (and adding the third of the chord), over a double-4th shape (root-eleventh-seventh) built from the root in the left hand.

- The A7(♯5,♯9) chord is voiced by building a major triad from the sharped fifth in the right hand, over a double-4th shape (seventh-third-sharped fifth) built from the seventh in the left hand.

- The G7(♯5,♭9) chord is voiced by building a minor triad from the flatted ninth in the right hand, over a double-4th shape (seventh-third-sharped fifth) built from the seventh in the left hand.

- The F13 chord is voiced by building a major triad from the root in the right hand, over a double-4th shape (seventh-third-thirteenth) built from the seventh in the left hand.

- The B7(♯5,♯9) chord is voiced by building a major triad from the sharped fifth in the right hand, over a double-4th shape (third-seventh-sharped ninth) built from the third in the left hand.

- The Cmaj9 chord is voiced by building a major triad from the fifth in the right hand, over a double-4th shape (third-sixth-ninth) built from the third in the left hand.

45

## FERMATA

A *fermata* is a sign over the music indicating a held note or chord, or a pause. This is often used at the end of a song to indicate that the last chord is held, as in the following pop ballad example.

TRACK 36

Pop ballad

Note the *fermata* signs used on the last D major chord, in the treble and bass clefs.

This example uses basic triads derived from the chord symbols in the right hand, over open-triad arpeggios in the left hand. As in most ballad styles, make sure that you depress the sustain pedal for the duration of each chord.

## FINDING A TEACHER

If you want to study in order to improve your musical skills, there are three basic paths you can take.

1) Self-study using instructional books/CDs/DVDs

2) Private lessons with a teacher in your area

3) Group lessons or classes at a community college, music trade school, or other institution

Of all the people around the world who use my music instruction books and CDs, the majority do so on a self-study basis. However, many people prefer to work with a teacher to get one-on-one guidance and to stay focused and motivated. Here are some ways to find a private teacher.

1) Call or visit your local music store and ask for teacher referrals. Many stores will have an approved "teacher list," which will often include people working at the store. Some stores also offer lessons and classes on the premises.

2) Call your local college or university (or music school, if there is one in your area) for recommendations.

3) Check local newspapers, bulletin boards, and the Yellow Pages.

Here are some other issues to bear in mind when evaluating private teachers and lessons.

1) **Location**: Decide whether you need somebody to come to your house, or whether you are able to travel to the teacher. Most established/experienced teachers will require you to travel to their studios.

2) **Duration and frequency**: Decide how long a lesson you need (for example, a typical arrangement might be one one-hour lesson per week). I only teach adult students, and I find that it's hard to get anything worthwhile accomplished unless the lesson lasts for at least an hour. Of course, for children a shorter lesson—perhaps half an hour—normally works better, due to attention span and other issues.

3) **Price**: Lesson rates will start at around $40 per hour for a private instructor (2007 figures). However, this figure may rise substantially depending on the teacher's experience and reputation. Don't be coerced into paying for a whole series of lessons in advance, before you've had a chance to evaluate the teacher properly.

4) **References**: It is perfectly appropriate to inquire about other people whom the teacher has instructed (or schools/institutions where the teacher has worked), and to get references. I tend not to get this type of inquiry very much, as most of my students have either bought my music instruction books in stores here in L.A., or come via personal recommendation. However, most teachers out there won't have the profile that I'm lucky enough to have, so make sure you find out as much as you can about the teacher before committing yourself.

5) **Qualifications**: Make sure the teacher is qualified (and I don't just mean the certificates he or she may have on the wall!) to teach the style(s) you are interested in. For example, I specialize in contemporary pop and jazz styles, and I don't teach classical music—so when I get inquiries from people who want classical lessons, I refer them to someone else. Your teacher should be an expert in the areas you need!

# FLASHCARDS

Obviously, it is very important for all piano players to know the notes in the treble and bass clefs (collectively referred to as the grand staff). Most music is notated within a two-octave span on either side of middle C, so you should make it a goal to learn and memorize all the notes in the following four-octave range:

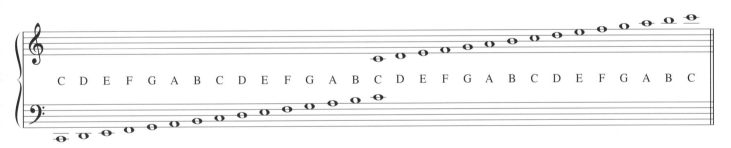

The best way to do this is to use *flashcards*, together with sightreading exercises appropriate for your level. A set of flashcards contains a card for each note in the treble and bass clefs, showing the notation (how the note is written) on the front, and the note name and keyboard location on the back. Work through the cards one at a time, and see how quickly you can name and/or find each note on the keyboard. If there are particular notes that you have difficulty with (for example, many beginners are slower to learn the bass-clef notes), then create a separate stack of these particular cards and work more on them.

Sets of flashcards are available at most music stores, and may also include cards showing different rhythmic values and other aspects of notation and harmony—a simple, yet very effective learning tool!

# FUNK

*Funk* is an American music style that emerged in the 1970s (within the overall family of R&B styles), and this style still has a large footprint in the twenty-first century. Funk music can be instrumental or vocal-based, and has a heavy emphasis on groove and syncopation. Most funk tunes use sixteenth-note rhythms, as does our first example.

This type of keyboard part is typical of funk styles, and sounds best when played with an electric piano or clavinet sound. Note the rhythmic conversation between the hands, within the framework of the left hand landing on beat 1 and the right hand landing on beats 2 and 4 (the backbeats).

## CHORD VOICING TIPS

This example mostly uses "7-3" voicings (the sevenths and thirds of the chords) in the right hand, alternating with a half-step leading tone into the lowest note. For example, on the Cm7 chord in measure 1, the "7-3" voicing has B♭ on the bottom, alternating with A (a half step below B♭). This is a signature funk sound.

The right hand is also using upper-structure and other devices as follows:

- On the Cm7 chords, the other 4th (C-F) is derived from the C minor pentatonic scale.

- On the B♭13sus4 chords, a major-seventh shape is built from the seventh (A♭maj7/B♭) and a minor triad is built from the fifth (Fm/B♭).

- On the final Cm7 chord, a major triad is built from the third (E♭/C).

Next up we have an example using a swing-sixteenths rhythmic feel—like the one on **Track 8** (p. 10)—typical of funk shuffle styles.

TRACK 38

Funk shuffle

Again, note the rhythmic interplay between the hands, this time using a more consistent eighth-note rhythmic pattern in the right hand, apart from the anticipations of beat 1. The left hand is playing the roots of the chords on beats 1 and 3, and other chord tones (fifths and sevenths) in the rhythmic gaps between the right-hand figures.

## CHORD VOICING TIPS

In this example the right hand is using upper structures, alternating triads, and modal harmony as follows:

- On the Dm7 chords, we are alternating between major triads built from the third (F/D) and seventh (C/D).

- On the B♭maj9 chord, we are alternating between major triads built from the fifth (F/B♭) and ninth (C/B♭).

- On the G9 and E♭9 chords, the voicings are based on four-part minor-seventh-flatted-fifth chord shapes built from the third (Bm7♭5/G and Gm7♭5/E♭), with additional passing tones from the G and E♭ Mixolydian modes.

- On the C13sus4 chords, the voicing is based on a four-part major-seventh chord shape built from the seventh (B♭maj7/C), with the additional passing tones coming from the C Mixolydian mode.

- On the Fmaj9 chords, the voicing is based on a four-part minor-seventh chord shape built from the third (Am7/F), with the additional passing tones coming from the F major scale.

- The A7alt symbol implies that all dominant chord alterations (♭5, ♯5, ♭9, ♯9) are available. The main root-flatted fifth-seventh voicing alternates with the third and sharped fifth of the chord, with the flatted ninth added during beat 4.

## FURTHER READING

For more information on funk keyboard styles, please check out a couple of my other books: *R&B Keyboard: The Complete Guide with CD!* and *The Pop Piano Book*, both published by Hal Leonard Corporation.

# GIG PREPARATION

Preparation is key to the success of your next gig, whether you're performing pop, jazz, or classical music. Here are some tips "from the trenches" on how to be prepared, and how to get the best out of the gig.

1) **Be ready to play**: Make sure that you've gone over your parts, not just in rehearsal with the band, but during your own practice time. When preparing for a gig with my original jazz fusion band, I'll try to play through our whole set on the three or four consecutive days before the gig, either solo piano or with backing tracks/sequences that I have prepared. As my band members are in-demand guys, sometimes we only get minimal rehearsal time, so everyone has to come to the gig prepared. If you're on a "chart gig" and you have the music ahead of time, scan through the tunes before the gig, making sure you know the road map and form of each song, and so on. If you're reading music at a classical recital, again, make sure you've had sufficient practice time with the music, and that all of your page-turns are okay. One exception to all this, of course, is if you're just showing up to a jam session, in which case you're winging it using your playing skills and your ears!

2) **Make sure your equipment is ready**: If you're just showing up to a jazz gig or classical recital, and will be playing the piano that is already there, you can skip to next section.... Otherwise, always make sure your equipment is in good working order and that you have all of the components you need. I have a checklist that I run down for keyboards, amplifiers, speakers, pedals, cables, plugboards, extensions, and so on—*before* I leave for the gig. *Always* carry spare cables (audio, MIDI, a/c mains, mic cables, etc.). If one of your keyboards or some other equipment has a technical problem, *never* use it on the gig in the hope that it will "behave itself"—that's a disaster waiting to happen. Get it fixed, and use another piece of equipment (perhaps a rental or loaner) in the meantime.

3) **Be punctual**: This sounds simple and obvious, but it's extremely important. If you get to the gig in plenty of time, you're likely to be more relaxed when you set up, and you'll have more time to deal with any curve balls thrown at you during the setup, soundcheck, and so on. Allow even more time to get to the gig if it's a venue you're playing for the first time, so that you can find the place, sort out the equipment load-in, parking, etc. When playing with my own jazz fusion band or with my Steely Dan tribute band in the Los Angeles area, I generally get to the gig two to three hours before showtime, depending on the particular setup and logistics involved (and I have to allow for the L.A. traffic!).

4) **Be relaxed and have a pleasant attitude**: Less experienced players will sometimes suffer from nervousness or stage fright when performing in public. Well, players of all levels will experience "nerves" from time to time; the trick is to get that nervous energy to stimulate you into giving a great performance, instead of holding you back. Especially if you're just starting out, try to get some family or friends to come to the gig and support you; then if an anxious moment strikes, you can look around and be comforted by familiar faces who want you to do well! We're always our own worst critics when it comes to our performance, but your audience will still most likely enjoy it and have a good time (provided you *keep going*). Always be very courteous and have a pleasant attitude toward your bandmates, the engineer(s), the venue staff, and any audience members you come into contact with. If you project a relaxed and sunny attitude, it will influence those around you—to everybody's benefit.

**G**

# GIG PROMOTION

So now that you've got that all-important gig for your band, how are you going to promote it so that people attend? Well, here are some *gig promotion* techniques you should know about.

1) **Internet**: Most bands I know have their own websites (i.e., www.yourband.com) and/or MySpace pages (i.e., www.myspace.com/yourband). Make sure your upcoming shows are posted on your website. If you haven't yet set up a MySpace page, make sure you register for an artist account rather than a general account. This will give you the MySpace artist functions (you can upload four of your songs for visitors to hear, list your upcoming shows, and so on). You can also set up a separate MySpace event to publicize your gig. If you're prepared to put in the time and effort to expand your MySpace friends network, send messages to people about your shows, and update your blog regularly with pictures, videos, and audio tracks, this can be an effective way to get people to your shows. If you haven't yet established your own band website, you can do so easily at www.hostbaby.com (run by the same folks as www.cdbaby.com, a leading online store for independent CDs). Their online "setup wizard" is easy to use: just type in your text and upload your photos and audio, and then choose a look from their various design templates. You don't need to be a web designer, there are no upfront costs, and the monthly fee is low. My own band site is hosted by Hostbaby; check us out at www.markharrisonquintet.com.

2) **Email**: Most bands these days send out one or more emails to everyone on their email list to promote each gig. Make sure you collect email addresses whenever you can (i.e., with sign-up sheets at your gigs, when selling your CDs, etc.). These days everybody gets tons of email, so try to make your gig emails stand out—for example, by including pictures as well as text. You might also consider combining your email list with those of other bands that you know, in order to reap the benefits of the combined list. (A cool feature of the Hostbaby site mentioned above is an email list manager for gig promotion.)

3) **Papers/magazines**: Check out the free papers in your area to see if there are listings of club gigs. For example, here in Los Angeles we have the *LA Weekly*, which has club listings by genre (rock, jazz, blues, etc.) for each night of the week. If the club is providing this information to the paper, make sure they have all the correct details about your band. If not, you can submit this information to the paper yourself. Depending on your budget, you might also consider paying for a display ad promoting your show. Make sure they run this in the same area of the paper as the gig listings, and if possible give them camera-ready artwork to use, as you will get more predictable results (and possibly a cheaper price).

4) **Snail mail**: Even in this email age, some bands still send out flyers or postcards promoting their shows. This is more costly than email, of course, but may stand more chance of getting the recipient's attention. This may be worth doing if you have names and addresses of some good prospects (for example, from CD sales). Also, people change their email addresses more often than their bricks-and-mortar addresses, so your snail-mail list may be more reliable.

5) **Flyers in the club**: Normally around two weeks before a club gig with my own band, I go into the club and put up posters promoting our show. This can be useful, as they will be seen by people who already go to the club. The flyers should show the band name and photo, the gig date and time, the cover charge (if applicable), and band website and/or MySpace page. You can also post flyers in the surrounding area if there are any suitable locations.

Good luck with promoting your gigs!

# GOSPEL

*Gospel* music originated in southern African-American churches in the early twentieth century as a combination of hymns, spiritual songs, and Southern folk music, bound together with religious lyrics of joy and celebration. Gospel styles have also blended with other styles (notably creating country gospel and blues gospel). Blues, country, and gospel collectively created the foundation for rock 'n' roll to emerge in the 1950s.

Traditional gospel frequently uses either an eighth-note triplet subdivision at a slow-to-medium tempo (think "Amazing Grace"), or sixteenth-note rhythms and syncopations at a faster tempo (as in the Paul Simon gospel standard "Gone at Last"). Here is our first example, in a slow gospel 3/4 style:

**TRACK 39**

This example uses an eighth-note triplet subdivision within a 3/4 time signature. (In fact, you may sometimes see the alternate time signature of 9/8—nine eighth notes per measure—used to notate this type of music.) Normally, both hands "lock up" on beat 1, with rhythmic variations (the hands either together or alternating) in the remainder of the measure.

## CHORD VOICING TIPS

In this example, the right hand is using upper structures and modal harmony as follows:

- On the G7 chords in measures 1 and 8, the four-part right-hand voicing is a combination of a major triad built from the root (G/G: top three notes) and a diminished triad built from the third (Bdim/G: bottom three notes).

- Elsewhere, on the first G7 chord, we are using Bdim, C, and Dm triads in the right hand (all from the G Mixolydian mode), and a four-part minor-seventh-flatted-fifth chord shape built from the third (Bm7♭5/G).

- The C7 chord is voiced by building a diminished triad from the third (Edim/C), and the passing F major triad on the last sixteenth note of beat 4 also comes from the C Mixolydian mode.

- The C♯dim7 chord is voiced with different inversions of the basic four-part chord (a common gospel sound).

- The first and last triads used over the D7 chord are Bm and Am (both coming from the D Mixolydian mode), and the chromatic passing triad in between is a B♭m triad (another signature gospel device).

- On the G/D chord, the movement between the upper G and C major triads is another example of backcycling (IV-I triad movements within the chord), as encountered on **Track 16** (p. 17).

The next example is in a fast gospel style, using sixteenth-note rhythms and anticipations.

**TRACK 40**

Fast gospel (4/4 time)

Note the exciting cross-rhythms created between the hands in this example. The left hand provides a steady eighth-note pulse using octaves, except during beat 2 of each measure where the left hand plays on the first two sixteenth notes in the beat, leading into the right-hand voicing halfway through beat 2 (the "and" of 2). Also, the right-hand voicings on the last sixteenth of beat 1 and the second sixteenth of beat 4 are very effective syncopations that land in between the left-hand octaves.

## CHORD VOICING TIPS

In this example, the right hand is using upper structures and modal harmony as follows:

- On the A7 and G7 chords, the first voicing is the same as the first G7 voicing in the previous example (a combination of major and diminished triads, resulting in the seventh-third-fifth-root of the chord from bottom to top).

- Elsewhere, all the upper triads come from the Mixolydian modes, built from the root of each chord. For example, on the A7 chord the C#dim, D, and Em triads all come from A Mixolydian; on the G7 chord the Bdim, C, and Dm triads all come from G Mixolydian, and so on.

## FURTHER READING

For more information on gospel piano techniques, please check out my *Gospel Keyboard Styles*, published by Hal Leonard Corporation.

# GRACE NOTES

A *grace note* is a note of very short duration that is "squeezed in" before another note. This type of right-hand ornamentation is very useful across a range of contemporary styles. Here's an example using grace notes, in a Nashville-era country style.

TRACK 41

You can see that the grace notes are much smaller than the "real" notes on the staff (for example, in measure 1 of the right hand, the E right before beat 2). Also the grace notes have no rhythmic value in the notation (i.e., if the grace note were removed from measure 1, the remaining notes and rests would still add up to four beats).

This traditional country pattern is a variation on the pentatonic scale techniques we saw in **Track 23** (p. 28). On the D major chord in measure 1, we are using a D pentatonic scale, moving between E and F# below an upper drone on A. The 4ths at the end of the measure (B-E and A-D) also come from this scale. Similarly, on the G major chord in measure 2, a G pentatonic scale is being used, and so on.

Note that the right hand is anticipating the D major triad leading into measures 3 and 8, and is also moving between E and F# during beat 4 of measures 2 and 7. This can be understood as ninth-third movement within the D major chord (these two notes are also found in a D pentatonic scale). The left hand is mostly playing a root-fifth pattern on each chord, typical of mainstream country styles.

## HALF NOTES AND RESTS

A *half note* lasts for two beats. This is equivalent to half a measure in 4/4 time. Here is an example of how half notes are written.

The rhythmic counting (1 2 3 4) is shown below the notes in this measure.

1 – 2    3 – 4

The half note is written as a white (or empty) notehead, with a stem attached.

Next we'll see an example of a half rest (which also lasts for two beats).

Here's a notation example that uses some half notes and rests.

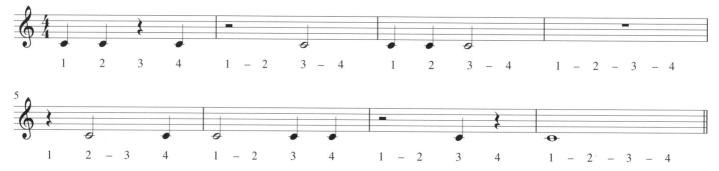

Note that the rhythmic sum of all the notes and rests in each measure agrees with the time signature (i.e., four beats in each 4/4 measure).

For information on other basic rhythmic values, see *Eighth Notes and Rests* (p. 38), *Quarter Notes and Rests* (p. 95), *Sixteenth Notes and Rests* (p. 104), and *Whole Notes and Rests* (p. 121).

## HALF STEP

The *half step* is the smallest unit of interval measurement in conventional Western music. If we move from any note on the keyboard to the nearest key to the right or left, this movement is a half step. Here are some examples of half steps.

Half steps may occur between white keys and/or black keys as follows:

- The half step C-D♭ is between a white key and a black key.

- The half step E-F is between two white keys that do not have a black key in between.

- The half step G♯-A is between a black key and a white key.

- The half step B-C is again between two white keys that do not have a black key in between.

Half steps and whole steps are the most common building blocks used when creating scales. Another important relationship to know is that there are twelve half steps per octave.

# HAND POSITION

*Hand position* (not surprisingly!) refers to the position of the hands on the keyboard. When playing simple songs, one or both hands might remain in the same position throughout. However, once you are playing songs beyond the beginner level, you will often need to move your hands to different positions on the keyboard. Here are some basics concerning finger numbers and hand positions (go ahead and skip this section if you're beyond the beginner level!). First, here are the finger numbers for both hands.

The fingering numbers for both hands are:

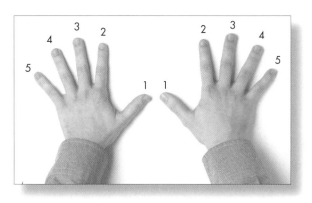

1  thumb

2  index finger

3  middle finger

4  ring finger

5  pinkie, or little finger

The following illustration shows a basic right-hand C-position, with the right thumb on middle C, and the pinkie on the G above.

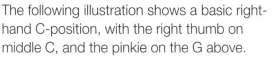

Here's a simple folk song that you can play entirely within this hand position. The finger numbers are shown above the staff.

"Go Tell Aunt Rhody" (Traditional)

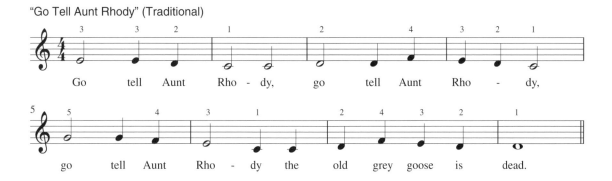

## FURTHER READING

For more information on hand positions, fingerings, and other beginner-level piano techniques, please check out my book and CD *All About Piano: A Fun and Simple Guide to Playing Keyboard*, published by Hal Leonard Corporation.

# IMPROVISATION

*Improvisation* occurs when a musician creates a part spontaneously (that is, without reading or having memorized it in advance). In contemporary styles, there are normally two general contexts in which this term is used.

1) If a keyboardist is spontaneously creating a complete part—whether comping or playing the melody together with the harmonization—the process can be referred to as improvisation, or playing by ear, or faking it.

2) If a keyboardist is extemporizing a single-note right-hand melodic line over a chord progression, this is also referred to as improvising, or *soloing*. In this case, the chord voicings might be played by the keyboardist's left hand and/or the rest of the band.

Both of these types of improvisation occur within contemporary pop and jazz styles. Here are some further observations on how improvisation might apply in different musical genres.

**Classical**: Except in certain experimental or "fringe" situations, you are expected to play the notes that are on the page (either by reading the actual music, or by memorizing it before-hand). Improvisation (adding your own notes, or changing what is written) is not appropriate, which is ironic given that many classical composers were also noted improvisers. Classical pianists do, however, have major interpretive responsibilities in areas such as dynamics, articulation, phrasing, and tempo. Through this interpretation process, the performer's musical personality will emerge.

**Jazz and Latin**: The majority of jazz compositions are written with just a melody and chord symbols. With the exception of some of the more "highly arranged" contemporary jazz styles, the chord voicings and melody phrasings are normally improvised by the players. Solos, in particular, will be improvised on the spot, and true jazz performers would never play a solo the same way twice (although they might have favorite phrases or "licks" that recur often in their solos). Latin styles such as bossa nova and samba would also come under this general heading, as they typically use the full range of jazz melody and harmony options, and have a similar approach in terms of improvisation.

**Pop/rock/R&B**: The majority of contemporary pop, rock, and R&B songs are performed within a specific structure or form (intro, verse, chorus, etc.). Most bands playing these styles are performing from memory, although some may be reading from leadsheets or fakebooks. There is not normally very much improvisation, except for instrumental solos—and even then the solo may be a recognizable signature that is played the same way each time. Yet, some rock bands do incorporate more extended improvisational jams—notably the Grateful Dead and the Dave Matthews Band.

## INTERPRETING CHORD PROGRESSIONS

In *Comping* (p. 24) and *Faking It* (p.43), we saw various examples of how chord symbols could be interpreted in contemporary styles. Now we'll look at how a single chord progression might be realized in different styles. Here's the progression we'll be using for this section:

## CHORD CHART

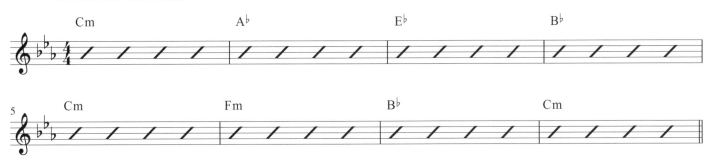

The chart consists of just chord symbols and slashes without a melody, which tells you to comp in the appropriate style. Our first interpretation is in a driving eighth-note pop/rock style.

TRACK 42

The right hand is using a mix of 4ths, alternating triads, and inverted double-4th shapes, with some rhythmic anticipations. The left hand is playing the chord roots in octaves, with eighth-note pickups into beat 3.

## CHORD VOICING TIPS

In measures 2, 4, and 6, this example uses alternating triads in the right hand, similar to **Tracks 13** and **14** (pp. 14–15).

- Alternating between major triads built from the fifth and the root, on the A♭ chord (adding the seventh and ninth).

- Alternating between major triads built from the seventh and the third, on the Fm chord (adding the seventh, ninth, and eleventh).

- Alternating between major triads built from the fourth and the root, on the B♭ chords. This interior IV-I triad movement is also known as backcycling, first introduced on **Track 16** (p. 17).

In measures 1, 3, and 5, this example uses 4ths derived from the C minor pentatonic scale (equivalent to the E♭ pentatonic scale) in the right hand. Also, at the start of measures 2 and 6, an inverted double-4th shape (B♭-E♭-A♭) has been built from the ninth of the A♭ chord and the eleventh of the Fm chord, respectively. This is a very useful sound in more advanced rock styles.

Next, we'll interpret the same progression in a New Age style. Here we want to create a dreamy or floating effect, with sustained right-hand voicings and light left-hand arpeggio patterns.

TRACK 43

The right hand is playing a mix of root-and-fifth voicings, basic triads derived from the chord symbols, and inverted double-4th shapes. The left hand is using open-triad arpeggio patterns, here adding the ninth of each chord (a signature New Age sound) on beat 2 of each measure.

Finally, we'll interpret the same progression in a sixteenth-note R&B/funk style.

TRACK 44

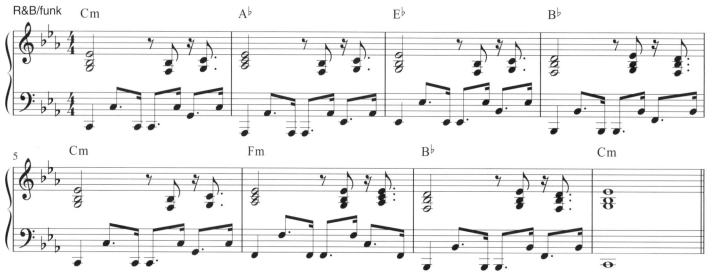

The right hand is playing a mix of upper triads and pentatonic 4ths, landing on beat 1, half-way through beat 3, and on the second sixteenth note of beat 4—a signature funk rhythmic figure. The left hand is playing the root and fifth of each chord, landing on all the downbeats, and with sixteenth-note pickups leading into beats 1, 3, and 4 of each measure. Note how the two hands land together on beat 1, and then "interleave" rhythmically during the remainder of each measure.

# INTERVALS

An *interval* is the distance between two notes. First of all, we'll take a look at the intervals created between the note C and the other notes in the C major scale (over a range of two octaves).

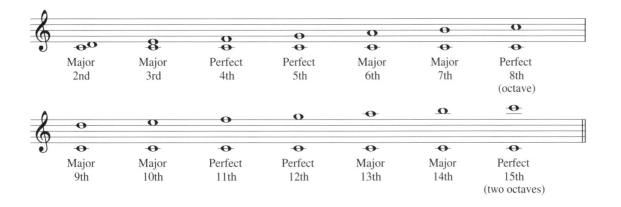

| Major | Major | Perfect | Perfect | Major | Major | Perfect |
|---|---|---|---|---|---|---|
| 2nd | 3rd | 4th | 5th | 6th | 7th | 8th (octave) |

| Major | Major | Perfect | Perfect | Major | Major | Perfect |
|---|---|---|---|---|---|---|
| 9th | 10th | 11th | 12th | 13th | 14th | 15th (two octaves) |

Note that each interval name contains a description (major, perfect) and a number (2nd, 3rd, 4th, etc.). The number part is easy to figure out: simply count up from the bottom note on the staff (starting at 1) until you reach the top note. For instance, looking at the major 3rd from the example above: the bottom note is C (1), the next note up on the staff would be D (2), and the next note up is E (3), which is the top note of the interval. The description will always be major or perfect if the top note of the interval is contained within the major scale built from the bottom note. As a quick rule of thumb, the 4ths, 5ths, and octaves (and these intervals plus one octave: i.e., 11th, 12th, etc.) are perfect, and the remaining intervals are major. Note that if we add or subtract the number 7 to/from an interval, we increase or reduce it by one octave (i.e., a 3rd plus an octave is a 10th: 3 + 7 = 10).

Some other descriptions apply when the above intervals are increased or reduced by a half step. Here is a summary of the rules you need to know.

- A major interval reduced by a half step becomes a minor interval.
  Example: C up to B is a major 7th, so C up to B♭ is a minor 7th.

- A minor interval reduced by a further half step becomes a diminished interval.
  Example: C up to B♭ is a minor 7th, so C up to B♭♭ is a diminished 7th.

- A major interval increased by a half step becomes an augmented interval.
  Example: C up to A is a major 6th, so C up to A♯ is an augmented 6th.

- A perfect interval reduced by a half step becomes a diminished interval.
  Example: C up to G is a perfect 5th, so C up to G♭ is a diminished 5th.

- A perfect interval increased by a half step becomes an augmented interval.
  Example: C up to F is a perfect 4th, so C up to F♯ is an augmented 4th.

Note that some of the above intervals are equivalent—i.e., the minor 7th (C-B♭) is equivalent to the augmented 6th (C-A♯). These intervals look the same on the keyboard (and sound the same, of course), but are written differently. Knowing all of these intervals makes spelling your triads and seventh chords a snap! Also note that the half step is equivalent to a minor 2nd, and the whole step is equivalent to a major 2nd.

# JAZZ

*Jazz* music has similar historical origins to the blues, in that it emerged in the late nineteenth century and then flourished and developed in the twentieth century. The main jazz styles and eras to develop are New Orleans and Dixieland (1910s–1920s), swing (1930s), bebop (1940s), cool jazz and post-bop (1950s), fusion (late 1960s–1970s), and contemporary jazz (1980s onwards). Jazz styles are noted for their improvisation and sophisticated harmony.

Our first jazz example is from the swing era, with four-part block voicings in the style of George Shearing.

TRACK 45

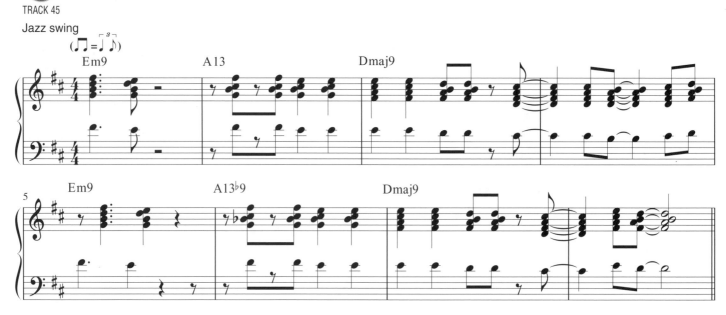

The right-hand voicings are mostly four-part upper structures on the various chords, and in this style the left hand is doubling the top note of the right-hand voicings, one octave lower. This means that the root of the chord is often not played in the piano part (that is, rootless voicings are being used). This example features typical jazz swing rhythms: i.e., anticipating beat 3 (measure 1), anticipating beat 1 (measures 4 and 8), and so on.

## CHORD VOICING TIPS

This jazz swing example uses upper-structure four-part chord shapes as follows:

- The Em9 chords are voiced by building a major-seventh shape from the third (Gmaj7/E) and a minor-seventh shape from the root (Em7/E).

- The A13 chord is voiced by building a major-seventh-flatted-fifth shape from the seventh (Gmaj7♭5/A) and a minor-seventh-flatted-fifth shape from the third (C♯m7♭5/A).

- The A13♭9 chord is voiced with two different upper structures:

  - a hybrid four-part shape (G-B♭-C♯-F♯) that is a combination of a diminished triad (Gdim: bottom three notes) built from the seventh, and a major triad (F♯: top three notes) built from the thirteenth

  - a diminished-seventh four-part shape built from the third (C♯dim7/A)

- The Dmaj9 chords are voiced by building a minor-seventh shape from the third (F♯m7/D), a minor-seventh shape from the sixth (Bm7/D), and a major-seventh shape from the root (Dmaj7/D).

Most jazz styles up to the 1950s used a swing-eighths rhythmic subdivision (as in the previous swing example). However, with the advent of fusion, straight-eighths rhythms began to appear. Our next example uses modal harmony in a straight-eighths rhythm, in the style of Herbie Hancock. This is typical of the jazz/rock fusion that was emerging by the late 1960s.

TRACK 46

These voicings are all derived from Dorian modes. In measures 1–4 and 9–12 on the Dm7 chord, the right hand is playing a repeated top note (or drone) of D above the moving triads Dm, Em, and F, which all come from D Dorian. The left hand is sustaining the root below a moving line that doubles the top note of each triad an octave lower. Similarly, on the E♭m7 chord, the right hand is playing E♭ as a drone above the moving triads E♭m, Fm, and G♭, which all come from E♭ Dorian. At the end of measure 12, we're using Cmaj7 and Dm7 four-part block shapes (again from D Dorian), in a style similar to that of the previous example.

## FURTHER READING

This tip gives you a brief glimpse into the vast world of jazz piano!

For more information on the history and development of jazz styles, as well as keyboard techniques for contemporary and smooth jazz, please check out my *Smooth Jazz Piano: The Complete Guide with CD!*; and for a comprehensive reference guide to the chords, voicings, and shapes used in jazz piano, see my *Contemporary Music Theory: Level Three*. Both of these books are published by Hal Leonard Corporation.

# JAZZ/BLUES

The paths of jazz and blues have been significantly intertwined, from the swing-band era of the 1930s to the fusion music of the 1970s and beyond. The term *jazz-blues* describes music combining jazz elements (rhythms, advanced harmonies, and improvisation) with blues elements (song form, melodic phrasing, blues scales).

Our first jazz-blues example has a twelve-measure blues form, but uses more sophisticated chords commonly found in mainstream jazz styles. This example is reminiscent of jazz/blues icons from the swing era, such as Count Basie and Duke Ellington.

TRACK 47

This example uses polychord (chord-over-chord) voicings, with typical jazz swing rhythms and anticipations.

## CHORD VOICING TIPS

This jazz/blues swing example uses filled-in octave voicings, triads, four-part chords, and double-4th shapes between the hands. Double 4ths here include shapes with a diminished 4th (equal to a major 3rd) on top.

- The C9 chords are voiced by playing one of the following in the right hand: the root in octaves (filled in with the fifth), a major triad built from the root, or a minor triad built from the fifth. These are all placed over a double-4th shape (third-seventh-ninth) built from the third in the left hand.

- The F13 chords are voiced by playing either the fifth in octaves (filled in with the ninth) or a double-4th shape (third-thirteenth-ninth) built from the third in the right hand, over a double-4th shape (seventh-third-thirteenth) built from the seventh in the left hand.

- The Gm7 chord is voiced by building a major triad from the third in the right hand, over a double-4th shape (root-eleventh-seventh) built from the root in the left hand.

- The C13 chords are voiced by building either a minor triad or a double-4th shape (thirteenth-ninth-fifth) from the thirteenth in the right hand, over a double-4th shape (third-seventh-ninth) built from the third in the left hand.

- The B♭13 chord is voiced by building a double-4th shape (seventh-third-thirteenth) from the seventh in the right hand, over a double-4th shape (third-seventh-ninth) built from the third in the left hand.

- The A7(♯5,♯9) chord is voiced by building a major triad from the sharped fifth in the right hand, over a double-4th shape (seventh-third-sharped fifth) built from the seventh in the left hand.

- The Dm11 chord is voiced by building a major triad from the seventh in the right hand, over a four-part major-seventh shape built from the third in the left hand.

- The G7(♯5,♯9) chord is voiced by building a four-part major-seventh-sharped-fifth chord shape from the third in the right hand, over a double-4th shape (seventh-third-sharped fifth) built from the seventh in the left hand.

- The G7(♭5,♭9) chord is voiced by building a four-part dominant-seventh shape from the flatted fifth in the right hand, over a double-4th shape (seventh-third-sharped fifth) built from the seventh in the left hand.

- The Dm9 chord is voiced by building a four-part major-seventh shape from the third in the right hand, over another four-part major-seventh shape built from the third in the left hand.

- The G7(♯5,♭9) chord is voiced by building a minor triad from the flatted ninth in the right hand, over a double-4th shape (seventh-third-sharped fifth) built from the seventh in the left hand.

The next example is typical of the driving soul/jazz style pioneered by Gene Harris in the 1960s. This was an exciting blend of jazz, blues, soul, and gospel influences.

TRACK 48

In this example the right hand is playing triads from Mixolydian modes in measures 1–6. For example, on the G7 chord in measure 1, the upper triads Dm, C, Bdim, and Am all come from the G Mixolydian mode. From measure 7, the right hand is playing basic upper shapes derived from the chord symbols, leading to a pair of seventh-third-thirteenth double-4th voicings on the A♭13 and G13 chords in measure 8. The left-hand octave pattern follows the root of each chord (on beat 1) with a scalewise or half-step line leading to the next chord.

### FURTHER READING

For more information on jazz/blues piano styles, please check out my *Jazz-Blues Piano: The Complete Guide with CD!*, published by Hal Leonard Corporation.

## JAZZ STANDARD

A *jazz standard* is a well-established tune in the jazz repertoire, played frequently by successive generations of performers. Standards have strong and enduring melodies, and they offer jazz musicians considerable potential for improvisation. Most jazzers will play standards either from memory or from a chart in a fake book. Try playing through this arrangement similar to a classic jazz standard.

TRACK 49

This example uses "7-3" voicings (the sevenths and thirds of the chords) below the melody, similar to the first half of **Track 35** (p. 44). Note the rhythmic phrasing and syncopations used (i.e., landing on the upbeats in measures 2, 4, and 6), all very typical of jazz swing styles.

The left hand is playing either the root of the chord, or a root-seventh interval. The root-seventh is a very common left-hand voicing in jazz styles, giving good support to the right hand. Don't play these intervals too low on the piano, or they will sound muddy—let your ears be the judge!

# KEEP GOING!

*Keep going*, no matter what happens. This applies to all performance situations and musical styles! Whether you're in the middle of Beethoven's "Moonlight Sonata," Coltrane's "Giant Steps," or the Beatles' "Lady Madonna," you should never stop if you fumble in mid-performance. Instead, you should keep going at all costs, striving to maintain the rhythm as consistently as you can. As musicians we always tend to be our own worst critics, but I guarantee you that the great majority of your audience will not notice those imperfections—provided that you keep going, and are "in the pocket" rhythmically. As I sometimes say in my classes: "If you keep going, maybe 2% of your audience will notice that you made a mistake. If you stop, then 100% of them will know!"

If you're on a pop or jazz gig and you lose your place in the form of the song, use your ears and try to figure out where the rest of the band is (i.e., are they on a I chord, the V chord, or somewhere else). At worst, if you're playing a tune with a repetitive form (like a jazz standard or a blues), try to catch up when the band returns to the top of the form again!

Refer also to the comments on "practicing the performance" in *Practice Habits* (p. 94).

# KEY SIGNATURES AND KEYS

A *key signature* is a group of sharps or flats at the beginning of the music that lets you know which *key* you are in (and which major scale to use). When we play the C major scale, we can hear that the note C sounds like the "home base" or *tonic* of the scale. If a song uses the C major scale, it is most likely to be in the key of C. As the C major scale contains only white keys, the key signature for C major contains no sharps and no flats.

When we build the F major scale, we need B♭ as the 4th degree of the scale. So the key signature of F major reminds you to play B♭ (instead of B♮) when playing in the key of F. That way we don't need to keep writing flat signs for every B♭ that comes up in the music.

Similarly, as the G major scale requires F♯ as its 7th degree, the key signature of G major reminds you to play F♯ (instead of F♮) when playing in the key of G.

Each of these key signatures also works for a minor key that is relative to the major key. If we re-position the C major scale to start on A (i.e., A-B-C-D-E-F-G-A), we get an A natural minor scale. This scale is used in the key of A minor, and the key signature would again have no sharps and no flats. The relative minor always begins on the 6th degree of the corresponding major scale: in our example, A is the 6th degree of the C major scale. So if you see a key signature with no sharps and no flats, how do you know if you're in the key of C major or A minor? Well, you have to make a contextual judgement in the music: for example, if the tonic were C, you would most likely be in C major; whereas if the tonic were A, you would be in A minor. Many tunes also move back and forth between the major and relative minor keys (several Beatles' songs—including "Yesterday"—do this). Here, for reference, are all of the major and minor key signatures:

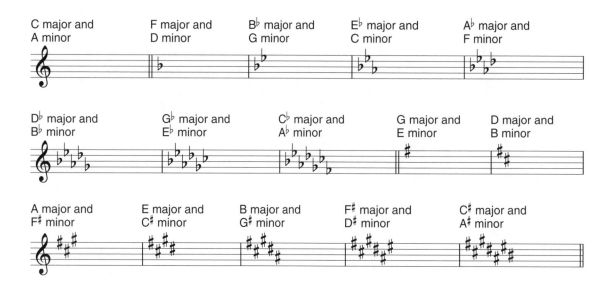

# L

## LEDGER LINES

*Ledger lines* are small staff lines placed above or below the staff in order to write notes that are too high or too low to be placed on the staff. Here is a grand staff showing all the Cs two octaves either side of middle C.

Middle C is a little above the bass clef, and a little below the treble clef. So we need to extend each clef (by adding a ledger line) to accommodate middle C. The Cs one octave above and below middle C are comfortably within each staff, but the Cs two octaves above and below middle C each need two ledger lines (above the treble staff, and below the bass staff).

As explained in *Flashcards* (p. 47), most piano music is written within this four-octave range—so the notes in this range are the most important ones to learn to recognize.

## LEFT-HAND PATTERNS

In most contemporary piano styles, the left hand needs to provide a consistent rhythmic foundation. This is especially true in blues styles, as the left hand propels the rhythm while also defining the harmonic progression. Our first *left-hand pattern* can be used across a range of blues, blues/rock, and shuffle styles.

TRACK 50

This example is based on dominant seventh chords within a basic twelve-measure blues form. The left-hand pattern uses root-fifth, root-sixth, and root-seventh intervals within each chord. You should play this with a steady, driving feel, and with a little extra emphasis on the downbeats. It's a good idea to learn this blues staple in as many keys as possible!

Next up we have a classic pop/rock groove, using the root of each chord in an octave pattern.

TRACK 51

Pop/rock

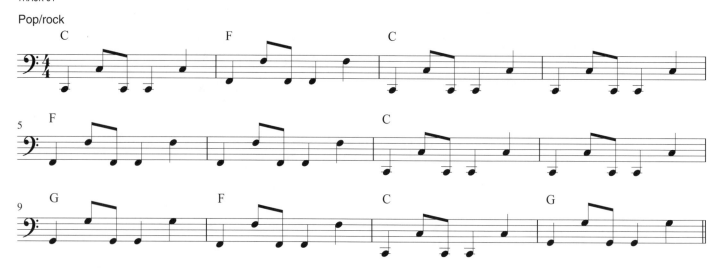

Note that this example uses the same twelve-measure form, this time with basic triad chord symbols. The left-hand pattern is imitating a pop-rock rhythm section, with the low root landing on beats 1 and 3 (where the kick drum and bass would typically lock up), and the high root landing on beats 2 and 4 (the backbeats where the snare drum would normally be played).

Our final left-hand pattern is in a quarter-note walking-bass style, suitable for jazz and jazz/blues tunes.

TRACK 52

Jazz-blues swing

Again, we are using the same form, this time with quarter notes on each downbeat (varied with eighth notes in measures 5 and 9). There are many ways to construct this type of walking bass line over chord changes. These general guidelines will get you started.

1) The root of the chord is almost always played on beat 1 of each measure, except when a chord continues into a second measure. In this case, other basic chord tones (i.e., third, fifth, or seventh) can be used on beat 1 of the second measure.

2) Once you know how high or low you want to play the root of the next chord, you can then design an ascending or descending line during the preceding measure, so as to lead into that root. These lines often have scalewise movement using Mixolyd-

ian modes (i.e., measure 4 descends using C Mixolydian), or chordal arpeggios (i.e., measure 2 ascends using the root, third, fifth, and thirteenth of the F7 chord).

3) Successive ascending or descending half steps are often used—for example in measures 3, 7, and 12 (ascending), and in measures 8, 10, and 11 (descending).

4) A half step is often used between beat 4 of a measure and the root of the next chord on the following beat 1 (for example, leading into measures 2, 9, 11, and 12). This kind of half-step approach is a signature sound in jazz styles.

# LEGATO PLAYING

To play *legato* means to play in a smooth and connected style (as opposed to *staccato*). This is normally indicated in the music by a slur, which is a curved line drawn across the musical phrase, from the first to the last note. *Legato playing* is commonly needed in ballad and New Age styles, as in the following example of a *legato* piano melody accompanied by strings.

TRACK 53

A couple of other interesting points to note about this example:

1) The string part uses open triads (the middle note of the triad has been transposed up an octave). This is an effective string arranging technique, and will help your synth strings to sound more realistic (as opposed to simply playing closed-position triads).

2) Note the slash chord symbols (i.e., Cm/G and Fm/A♭). This type of chord symbol is often used when a note other than the root (i.e., the third or fifth) is the lowest voice. In this case the Cm chord has its fifth (G) on the bottom, and the Fm chord has its third (A♭) on the bottom. This technique enables the lowest string voice to move by half steps, creating a smooth melodic effect.

# LIVE PERFORMANCES

As musicians, there are two types of *live performances* we are concerned with: either we are going to see someone else play, or we are performing ourselves. If you are seeing another band perform, you might be showing up to support some friends in the band (always appreciated!), and/or you may be seeing a top act that will inspire and motivate you in your own musical endeavors. Always try to make time to get out to live shows as often as you can. Here in Los Angeles I regularly interact with a lot of pro jazz players, and because there are great musicians playing club gigs here every night of the week, we bemoan the fact that the public is often apathetic and that it can be tough to get people out to shows! So, no matter where you live, check out your local gig listings and/or internet postings, and support live music—it's in everybody's best interest!

If you are performing yourself, you'll of course want to promote your show as effectively as you can; some suggestions for this are given in *Gig Promotion* (p. 52). If you are looking for live performance opportunities, the following guidelines should get you started:

## SOLO GIGS

If you are new to playing solo gigs, a good place to get started would be an open-mic session at a local club or coffeehouse, particularly if they have a piano already set up. The musicians at these events are mostly singer/songwriters, and you normally get to do one to three songs, depending on the time available.

A lot of clubs, bars, and restaurants have solo piano players, and most of them are also singers. The style of music will vary depending on the establishment. Check out the venues in your area, the musical styles they feature, and the nights of the week when they have music. You can inquire directly with the management at the club, or through their agent. Submit a promo pack with a brief bio, photo, and CD of your playing.

At a higher level of solo work, there is the hotel circuit. Some of my students have played at the Beverly Hills Hotel Polo Lounge, which is perhaps the best hotel gig in the Los Angeles area. These high-end gigs are normally found either by personal recommendation or referral, or through the hotel management or an agent. To have a shot at this type of gig, you need to be very personable and presentable, and have a good repertoire of pop and jazz standards, show tunes, and popular classical music.

## BAND GIGS

If your band plays original rock, you need to hit the clubs that cater to that world (in Los Angeles, that would be the rock clubs along the Sunset Strip, such as the Whisky and the Roxy). If you play pop/rock/R&B covers, this opens up a wider range of possibilities to play at clubs, bars, and restaurants, particularly on the weekends. Acoustic straight-ahead jazz normally finds a home in coffeehouses, bookstores, hotels, restaurants, and jazz clubs, while contemporary electric jazz is usually performed in clubs specifically dedicated to that style.

Tribute bands can also find work at rock clubs, which will sometimes have a "tribute-band night" (often on a weekend) featuring several groups on one bill. Outdoor events such as festivals, seasonal concerts, and arts-and-crafts shows are also options for cover bands, tribute bands, and jazz bands. These events are often coordinated by city offices or corporate sponsors. Also, some bands specialize in playing at private parties, weddings, and functions; to compete for this type of work, your repertoire, stylistic versatility, and appearance all have to be top-notch!

# MAJOR SCALE

The *major scale* is the most commonly used scale in Western music. Most famous melodies that you know are constructed from major scales. Like all scales, the major scale is a sequence of notes created using a specific set of intervals. Most scales (including the major scale) are created using half steps and whole steps, although some scales contain larger intervals. Here is a C major scale, showing the specific sequence of whole steps and half steps:

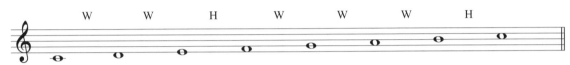

When we construct this pattern of intervals starting on the note C, we use all the remaining white keys on the keyboard. If we start this pattern of intervals from any other note, we'll end up with a mixture of white and black keys. The major scale is a seven-note scale (i.e., there are seven different pitches) that uses all the letter names in the musical alphabet consecutively (with no letter name being used more than once). Now we'll build this pattern of whole steps and half steps from F, to create the F major scale:

Notice that we now have the note B♭ as the 4th degree of this scale. This is because we need a half step between the 3rd and 4th degrees: we already have A as the 3rd degree, and we need to use the next consecutive letter name (B) for the next note, so we flat the B (to B♭) to get the required half step above A. Next, we'll use the same method to build a G major scale:

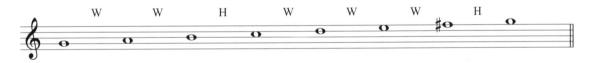

Notice that we now have the note F♯ as the 7th degree of this scale. This is because we need a whole step between the 6th and 7th degrees: we already have E as the 6th degree, and we need to use the next consecutive letter name (F) for the next note, so we sharp the F (to F♯) to get the required whole step above E.

*Key Signatures and Keys* (p. 67) gives the key signatures for these (and all other) major scales. I would recommend, however, that you learn to build your major scales by using the whole steps and half steps shown above (rather than using key signatures to figure them out), as this more closely parallels how your ear relates to the scale. In other words, your ear will recognize the pattern of whole steps and half steps from any starting note, but it doesn't care how many sharps or flats there are! Thus, I think it is better to build your scales in a way that your ear understands.

# MEMORIZING SONGS

In my classes I am sometimes asked about techniques for *memorizing songs*. Memorization is important if you are building up a repertoire, and in particular if you are playing function or casual gigs, where your stylistic versatility and fast transitions between tunes will mean they'll hire you rather than the next guy (or girl)! Also, musical style is a factor when deciding whether the music should be memorized. For example, on jazz gigs it is generally acceptable for musicians to read charts, but on rock gigs the musicians normally play from memory (having charts onstage is not compatible with the energy and vibe of rock music, and in any case most rock musicians play by ear). When I perform with my contemporary jazz quintet here in L.A., I'll take charts for any cover tunes we're doing, but when I perform with my Steely Dan tribute band (which is a rock gig, albeit more sophisticated than the typical rock gig), I have everything memorized.

In contemporary styles, the key to memorizing songs is not to memorize the whole keyboard arrangement (with the exception of any signature parts essential to the song), but rather to memorize the melody, chord changes, and form (i.e., the different sections of the tune, how many measures in each section, etc.). In other words, memorize the information that would be on a chart or leadsheet. Then you can play the voicings and rhythms in a more spontaneous way when you perform the song, as discussed in *Faking It* (p. 43). That way you'll be memorizing less data per song, which should enable you to memorize more songs more quickly! The musical style will influence the degree to which your performance will vary from one gig to the next, as you recall this basic information for each song. For example, on a jazz gig you are more likely to interpret the same song differently each time, whereas in pop or rock styles you're more likely to perform the song in a similar way from one gig to the next.

# MIDI

*MIDI* stands for "musical instrument digital interface." This is a protocol by which keyboards, computers, and other pieces of equipment communicate with each other. You can think of MIDI data as a digital piano roll, containing information about which notes are played, their durations, volumes, and so on. When MIDI technology first appeared back in the 1980s, there was great excitement at being able to play one keyboard while hearing the sounds from another (having connected them with a MIDI cable). This is all very routine today, of course— but back then it was pretty revolutionary.

MIDI technology has several uses. Here is a summary of some of the more common ones for musicians performing live, and/or recording in a home studio.

1) Connecting the "MIDI out" from a controller keyboard to the "MIDI in" of another sound source: either another MIDI keyboard as described above, a MIDI rack module (essentially a synthesizer and/or sample playback device without a physical keyboard attached), or a MIDI rack computer device (such as the Muse Receptor) that enables you to play back plug-in and software instruments, as described in *Digital Audio Workstation* (p. 32). You can play the controller keyboard and hear the sound(s) of the attached keyboard or module. If your controller keyboard also has on-board sounds, you can then layer and blend the sounds between the different sources (this is what I do in my own live setup).

2) Connecting the "MIDI out" from a controller keyboard to the "MIDI in" of a MIDI interface connected to a Mac or PC (or in some cases, directly to the computer). This will then enable you to get MIDI data to and from your computer, which is useful in various ways, including the following:

a) If you are recording with digital audio workstation software, the MIDI data recorded from your controller can then be used to trigger any external MIDI synthesizer or device in your system and/or any plug-in synthesizers or software installed in your computer. The MIDI data can be edited and manipulated as needed in your workstation software, and this process can then be repeated for each track/instrument in your song.

b) If you are creating a chart or score with music-notation software, the MIDI data can be read by the software to produce the score. You'll still probably need to edit and refine the score further, but this is still much faster than creating the score from scratch. Most digital audio workstation software has notation capabilities; yet for maximum flexibilty and "publishing quality" notation, I prefer to use a dedicated notation program (Finale® and Sibelius are the two top contenders in 2007).

c) If you have acquired MIDI files that you wish to play back, and you don't want to use a standard MIDI-file player program or plug-in synths, you can route the MIDI data to any external MIDI device in your setup to hear the MIDI files play back on that particular device.

# MINOR SCALES

There are three *minor scales* in common usage: melodic, harmonic, and natural. Here we'll take a look at the intervals present in each, how we can alter a major scale to create each one, and how we might use them in minor-key situations.

First, we'll look at the C melodic minor scale, noting the whole steps and half steps used.

The melodic minor scale is widely used in jazz styles. If we were to take a C major scale and alter it to create a C melodic minor scale, we would lower the 3rd degree by half step (E becomes E♭). If we were to use the C melodic minor scale within a C minor key signature, we would contradict the key signature by raising the 6th and 7th degrees by half step (A♭ becomes A♮, and B♭ becomes B♮). Depending on the musical style, all minor scales may potentially be used in a minor key, which may then require accidentals (sharps or flats contradicting the key signature).

Next up is the C harmonic minor scale.

Note the unusual interval toward the top of this scale: a minor 3rd (equivalent to three half steps, or one-and-a-half steps). Melodically, this gives the scale a somewhat angular sound, which is exploited in various ethnic and Middle Eastern music. Harmonically, the scale is useful for deriving chords in jazz, in part due to the two half steps in the upper part of the scale. If we were to take a C major scale and alter it to create a C harmonic minor scale, we would lower the 3rd and 6th degrees by half step (E becomes E♭, and A becomes A♭). If we were to use the C harmonic minor scale within a C minor key signature, we would contradict the key signature by raising the 7th degree by half step (B♭ becomes B♮).

Our last scale is the C natural minor scale:

The natural minor scale is widely used in pop and rock styles, and is equivalent to an Aeolian mode (a major scale—E♭ major, in this case—re-positioned to start on its 6th degree). If we were to take a C major scale and alter it to create a C natural minor scale, we would lower the 3rd, 6th, and 7th degrees by half step (E becomes E♭, A becomes A♭, and B becomes B♭). If we were to use the C natural minor scale within a C minor key signature, no adjustments would be needed, as everything conforms to the key signature.

### FURTHER READING

For more information on the harmonic implications of the different minor scales, as well as their uses in minor keys, please check out my *Contemporary Music Theory: Level Two*, published by Hal Leonard Corporation.

# MIXOLYDIAN MODE

A mode (or modal scale) is created when we take a major scale and displace it to start on another scale degree. An example of this is the *Mixolydian mode*, created when the major scale is displaced to start on the 5th degree. The following example shows a C major scale displaced to create a G Mixolydian mode.

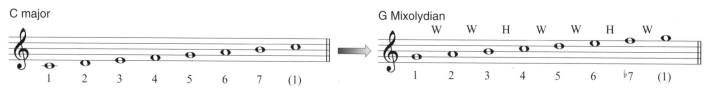

If you compare these two scales, you'll see that the notes are the same; they just begin and end in a different place. Thus each has a different tonic and a different pattern of whole and half steps. You can also think of the Mixolydian mode as a major scale with a flatted 7th degree (1-2-3-4-5-6-♭7). This mode has a dominant sound and is a basic scale source for a dominant seventh chord. We could say that C major is the relative major scale of G Mixolydian, as C major was the scale originally displaced to create the mode.

To use a Mixolydian mode harmonically, we would simply put the tonic of the mode (G in the above example) in the bass, and then place notes and/or chords from the mode (or from its relative major) above this bass note. A common tactic is to use diatonic triads from the relative major. For example, the diatonic triads in C major are C, Dm, Em, F, G, Am, and Bdim. Placing any of these above the tonic G is an effective way to create Mixolydian harmony.

Our first example is in a swing-sixteenths funk or hip-hop style, and uses triads from the C, B♭, A♭, and F Mixolydian modes. For example, on the C7 chords we are using a mix of Edim, F, Gm, Am, and B♭ upper triads, all of which are diatonic to the F major scale (the relative major of C Mixolydian). Similarly, on the B♭7 chords we are using triads (Ddim, E♭, and F) from the B♭ Mixolydian mode (relative of the E♭ major scale), and so on.

TRACK 54

Hip-hop funk

Note the alternating sixteenth-note rhythms between the hands, typical of contemporary funk styles.

Next up we have a blues shuffle using Mixolydian modes and triads.

TRACK 55

Blues shuffle

This twelve-measure blues example uses D Mixolydian triads (F#dim, G, Am, Bm) over the D7 chord, then uses G Mixolydian triads (Am, G, F) over the G7 chord, and so on. Note the left-hand pattern that moves from the flatted third to the third of each chord during beats 2 and 4 of each measure. This is a signature sound in Chicago-style blues.

Also notice that both of these Mixolydian examples use a lot of inverted triads in the right-hand parts. Modal triads tend to sound better when inverted. Second-inversion triads are used the most, due to their strong and powerful sound.

For another important mode, see *Dorian Mode* (p. 33).

## MODAL SCALES

A *mode* (or *modal scale*) is created when we take a major scale and displace it to start on another scale degree. We'll use the C major scale as the basis for these examples. The mode name given to an undisplaced major scale (i.e., a major scale starting on its regular tonic) is Ionian.

**C major** (or C Ionian)

This scale can then be displaced to start on other scale degrees, creating the following modes.

**D Dorian** (C major scale starting from its second degree)

**E Phrygian** (C major scale starting from its third degree)

**F Lydian** (C major scale starting from its fourth degree)

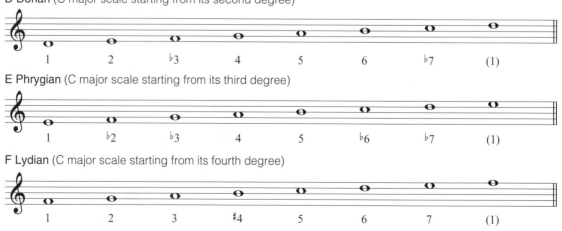

G Mixolydian (C major scale starting from its fifth degree)

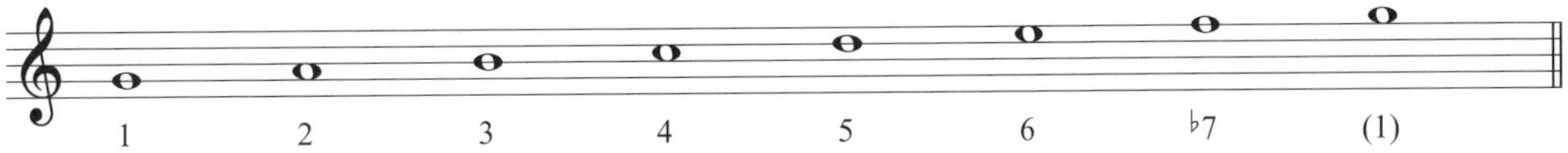

1  2  3  4  5  6  ♭7  (1)

A Aeolian (C major scale starting from its sixth degree)

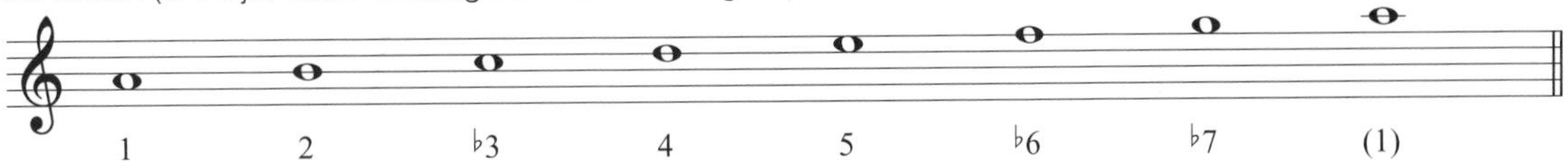

1  2  ♭3  4  5  ♭6  ♭7  (1)

B Locrian (C major scale starting from its seventh degree)

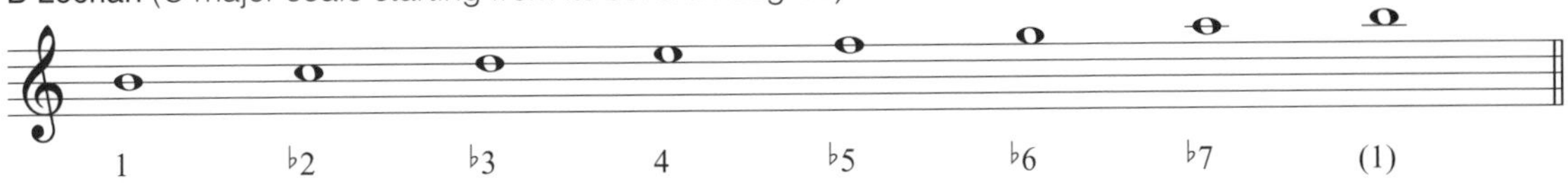

1  ♭2  ♭3  4  ♭5  ♭6  ♭7  (1)

Modal scales (especially the Dorian and Mixolydian) are widely used in contemporary music. The more angular sounds of the Phrygian and Locrian modes (which both start with a half step) are generally reserved for jazz and other more sophisticated styles.

# NEIGHBOR TONES

*Neighbor tones* are embellishments added to a melody or solo line, which lead into another note by a whole step or half step. First of all, we'll see how to add neighbor tones to a melody in a basic country/pop style.

TRACK 56

The first eight measures show the melody without neighbor tones. In the last eight measures the same melody is repeated, this time with neighbor tones added. In this simple country style, the neighbor tones are *grace notes*, most a whole step away from the main note. The melody is derived from pentatonic scales (i.e., G pentatonic over the G chord, C pentatonic over the C chord, etc.), and the neighbor tones can also be derived from these scales. In this style, neighbor tones (sometimes referred to as "hammers") are typically of short duration.

The next example applies neighbor tones when improvising in a jazz swing style. When soloing over chord changes, one of the various techniques available is to use arpeggios. We can then add neighbor tones to these arpeggios for further variation and interest. This example uses a II-V-I progression (four-part chords built from the 2nd, 5th, and 1st degrees of the key), which is a staple sound in mainstream jazz styles. The first eight measures show just the arpeggiated chord tones, which we will use as our *target notes*, a framework for embellishment. The last eight measures then show upper and lower neighbors built around these chord tones. In this jazz swing style, the upper neighbors are normally diatonic to the key (in this case C major), but the lower neighbors can always move by half step. For example, in measure 10 the A (fifth of the Dm7 chord) is preceded by the upper neighbor B and lower neighbor G♯ during beat 4 of the previous measure. B is a diatonic upper neighbor, while G♯ is a chromatic lower neighbor (i.e., it is not contained within a C major scale). The extra "leading" quality of these half steps is a signature jazz improv sound.

TRACK 57

Jazz/swing

There are, of course, many rhythmic re-phrasing possibilities here. Try applying some eighth-note anticipations, and don't forget to swing the eighth notes!

# NEW AGE

*New Age* is an American instrumental music style that emerged in the 1980s, with an emphasis on calming sounds and the avoidance of harsh textures. Most piano-based New Age music uses arpeggios in the left and/or right hands at slow-to-medium tempos, and often borrows from classical and smooth jazz styles. Our first New Age example uses two-handed arpeggios within an eighth-note rhythmic subdivision.

TRACK 58

New Age (eighths)

This example uses gently flowing arpeggios that begin in the left hand and continue with the right hand, anticipating beats 3 and 4 in each measure. Almost all New Age styles will require you to depress the sustain pedal for each chord (make sure you release the pedal at the point of chord change). Note the very open and transparent sound that results from using the various double-4th voicings in the right hand.

## CHORD VOICING TIPS

This example uses the root and fifth of each chord in the left hand, with various double-4th (two consecutive 4ths) shapes and their inversions in the right hand, as follows:

- The $G^6/_9$ and $F^6/_9$ chords are voiced by building a double 4th from the sixth (E-A-D and D-G-C, respectively).

- The Csus2, Dsus2, and Gsus2 chords are all voiced by building double 4ths from the ninth (D-G-C, E-A-D and A-D-G, respectively) with some inversions and octave doubling.

- The $B\flat^6/_9$ chord is voiced by building a double 4th from the third (D-G-C).

The next New Age example uses a sixteenth-note rhythmic subdivision, and is again played in a very legato and flowing style. This time the right hand alternates between 5ths and 6ths in the various upper-structure triads. For example, in the right hand of measure 1 on the Dmaj9 chord, we have an A major triad (bottom to top: E-A-C#-E) split so that the A and the top E land on beat 1, and the C# and the bottom E land on the last sixteenth of beat 1. Splitting a triad (with the top note doubled an octave lower) into intervals this way is a common technique in ballad and New Age styles.

TRACK 59

New Age (sixteenths)

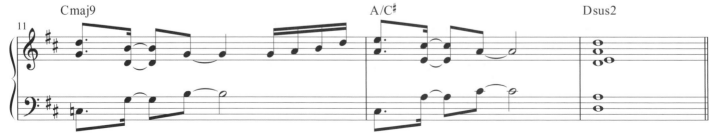

The left hand is playing open arpeggio patterns on each chord, similar to the open triads on **Track 63** (p. 86), but with some extensions added to the chords.

## CHORD VOICING TIPS

In this example, the right hand is using upper-structure triads (split into 5ths and 6ths) as follows:

- The Dmaj9, Cmaj9, and B♭maj9 chords are all voiced by building major triads from the fifth: A/D, G/C, and F/B♭.
- The B11 and A11 chords are voiced by building major triads from the seventh: A/B and G/A.

Also, the Dsus2 chord is voiced by building a double 4th from the ninth (E-A-D), with the D doubled an octave below.

The left hand is playing the following open arpeggio patterns:

- The Dmaj9, Cmaj9, and B♭maj9 chords all use a "1-5-7" pattern (D-A-C♯, C-G-B, and B♭-F-A).
- The B11 and A11 chords use a "1-5-9" pattern (B-F♯-C♯ and A-E-B).
- The G/B and A/C♯ chords use a "3-1-3" pattern (B-G-B and C♯-A-C♯).

# OCTAVES

An *octave* is the interval between a note and the next-occurring note of the same name, either higher or lower on the keyboard. Many contemporary styles make use of octave patterns in the left- and/or right-hand parts. Our first example using octaves is in a boogie-woogie style.

TRACK 60

This example uses octaves throughout the right-hand part, giving a strong and powerful sound. The chord progression is a basic twelve-bar blues in C, and the right-hand motifs are mostly derived from the C and A blues scales. A minor is the relative minor scale of C major, and it is common to use phrases from both the blues scales built from the tonic and the one built from the relative minor (i.e., the C blues scale and the A blues scale in the key of C). For example, in measures 1–2 the right-hand notes all come from the A blues scale, but in measures 3–4 the right-hand notes all come from the C blues scale. Meanwhile, the left hand is playing the root of each chord in octaves, before connecting the third to the fifth by half steps (E-F-F#-G on the C7 chord). This is all very typical of boogie-woogie and early blues styles.

Our next example is in a driving hard rock style, using octaves in both hands.

TRACK 61

**Hard rock**

Note that this example doesn't use any chords at all, just single lines in octaves. The chord symbols, however, are implied by the melody notes in conjunction with the bass line. The steady eighth-note pulse in the left hand is a common ingredient in pop/rock and hard rock styles.

Our last example is in a fast gospel style, using octaves within a swing-sixteenth-note rhythmic subdivision.

TRACK 62

**Fast gospel**

Note that while the C7 chord is implied throughout this example, there is considerable movement within the chord—which is typical of more sophisticated gospel music. The I-IV-I (C major-F major-C major) right-hand movement over beats 1–2 in measures 1, 3, 5, and 7 is an example of backcycling, a technique first encountered on **Track 16** (p. 17). Otherwise, the single-note lines in octaves are again derived from a mix of C and A blues scales. The left-hand octave pattern lands on the root of the chord (C) on beat 1 of each measure, and then either walks back up to the root in half steps (A-B♭-B♮-C) or up to the third in half steps (D-E♭-E♮). Make sure to catch the sixteenth-note anticipations in the right hand, as this is important to the style!

## OPEN TRIADS

An *open triad* is created when the middle note of a triad (whether in root position or inverted) is moved up or down by one octave. This creates an overall span, from the lowest to highest note, greater than one octave. We saw this technique used in *Legato Playing* (p. 71) to harmonize a melody with a string pad. In this section we will use open-triad arpeggios as a left-hand pattern in both eighth-note and sixteenth-note ballad styles. We'll apply these arpeggios to the same progression used on **Tracks 11** and **12** (p. 13), beginning with this eighth-note pop ballad example.

TRACK 63

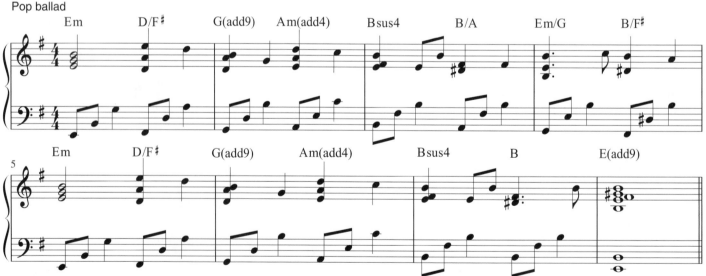

This example includes several chord symbols designating inverted harmonies in which a major or minor triad is placed over its third or fifth in the bass. Common open-triad left-hand patterns are: root-fifth-third when the chord symbol is not inverted (i.e., the Em chord); third-root-fifth when the triad is placed over its third in the bass (i.e., the D/F♯ chord); and fifth-third-root when the triad is placed over its fifth in the bass (i.e., the B/F♯ chord). The right-hand part is mostly a mix of triads, suspended chords, and add9 chords (note how the ninth resolves to the root in measures 2 and 6). Next, we'll see the same chord progression used with a sixteenth-note R&B ballad comping pattern.

TRACK 64

R&B ballad

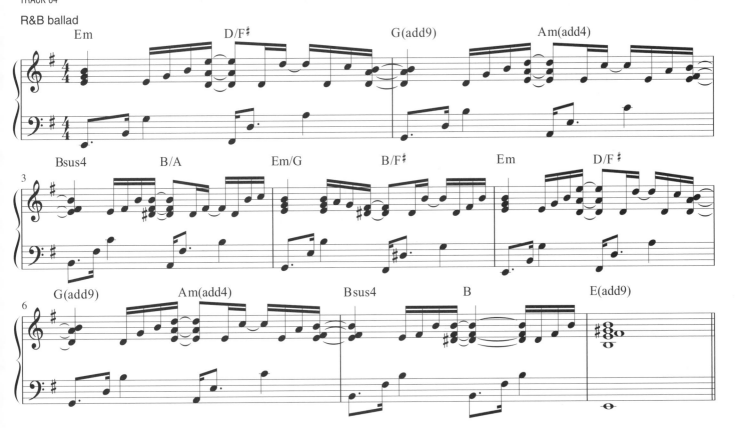

Here we see the voicings in the right hand anticipate beat 3 by a sixteenth note in most measures, which is typical of R&B ballads. The right hand is playing triads, suspensions, and added ninths similar to those in the previous example, now with some sixteenth-note arpeggios during beats 2 and 4. The left hand is playing the same open-triad arpeggios as in the previous example, now rhythmically re-phrased for the sixteenth-note style (the middle note of the arpeggio is placed on either the second or fourth sixteenth note of the beat).

# OSTINATO

An *ostinato* is a musical figure that is repeated throughout a section of a song (or sometimes throughout the *whole* song). In contemporary piano styles, ostinatos are often repeated against changing chords, and can occur in the left or right hands. Our first example uses an ostinato in the left hand, in an R&B dance/pop style.

TRACK 65

R&B dance/pop

The left-hand ostinato is a repeating two-measure phrase derived from an A minor pentatonic scale (A-C-D-E-G), placing the root of the Am7 chord on beat 1 and the root of the Dm7 chord on the last sixteenth note of beat 4 (anticipating the following downbeat) in measures 1, 3, 5, and 7.

## CHORD VOICING TIPS

In this example the right hand is using upper-structure triads as follows:

- The Am7 and Dm7 chords are voiced by building major triads from the third: C/A and F/D.

The next example uses a two-measure ostinato in the right hand, in a pop/rock style. This right-hand part uses a double-4th shape (G-C-F) in a combination of first and second inversions (C-F-G and F-G-C), creating a right-hand shape of C-F-G-C from bottom to top. Although this might just look like a Csus4 chord (which is indeed the result when placed over C in the bass, as in the first measure), this same shape creates some very interesting chord qualities when placed over different roots.

TRACK 66

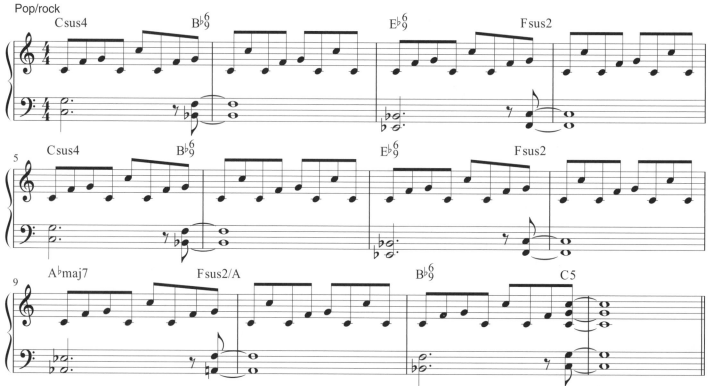

In this example the left hand is playing root-fifth intervals throughout (except for the third-root interval on the Fsus2/A chord), landing on beat 1 of the odd-numbered measures and anticipating beat 1 of all the even-numbered measures.

## CHORD VOICING TIPS

In this example the right hand's double-4th shape G-C-F (inverted and doubled to create the C-F-G-C right-hand voicing) has been built from the following chord tones:

- The fifth of the Csus4 chord
- The sixth of the B♭6/9 chord
- The third of the E♭6/9 chord
- The ninth of the Fsus2 (and Fsus2/A) chords
- The seventh of the A♭maj7 chord

# PENTATONIC SCALE

The *pentatonic scale* (sometimes referred to as "major pentatonic") is a five-note scale that is widely used in rock, country, and gospel styles. Here is an example of a G pentatonic scale.

TRACK 67
Part 1

G pentatonic scale

The G pentatonic scale contains the following notes (with intervals above the tonic G in parentheses): G, A (major 2nd), B (major 3rd), D (perfect 5th), and E (major 6th). This scale is equivalent to a major scale with the 4th and 7th degrees removed.

TRACK 67
Part 2

Here is an example, in a traditional 3/4 slow gospel style, that uses the pentatonic scale to create a fill.

In measure 2, the G pentatonic scale (G-A-B-D-E) is used in ascending octaves to connect between the G and C major chords. This is a very effective way to build energy and to change registers (the right-hand voicing on beat 1 of measure 3 is an octave higher than that on beat 1 of measure 2). Otherwise the right hand is playing triads (with octave doubling), and the left hand is playing a mix of intervals (root-fifth and root-sixth), octaves, and single notes.

### CHORD VOICING TIPS

In this example, the right hand is using backcycling and upper-structure triads as follows:

- On the G chord, the right hand is backcycling (alternating between I and IV triads).
- On the C chord, the right hand is alternating between a major triad built from the root (C), and a minor triad built from the sixth (Am).
- The D11 chord is voiced by building different inversions of a major triad from the seventh: C/D.

# PERSONAL DIGITAL STUDIO

A *personal digital studio* is a self-contained, portable hard-disk multitrack recorder, and can be thought of as the twenty-first-century successor to the tape-based Portastudio machines introduced in the 1980s. You can record parts from your favorite keyboard or synthesizer directly into the machine (by connecting the audio outputs from your keyboard to the audio inputs on the recorder). You can then record the piano part on track 1, bass on track 2, and so on. You can also record other non-keyboard instruments (guitar, sax, voice, etc.) with a microphone connected to the mic inputs. When you're done recording, you can then combine all the elements into a final mix and burn a CD. Some units will also have built-in drum loops and bass sounds to give you a head start with your rhythm section tracks.

Popular examples of personal digital studios in 2007 (manufacturers in parentheses) are:

## Budget:

BR-600 (Boss)

MRS-8 (Zoom)

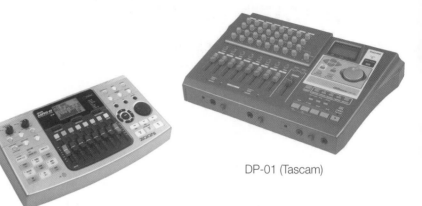

DP-01 (Tascam)

## Mid-range:

BR-1200CD (Boss)

BR-1600CD (Boss)

D3200 (Korg)

2488 MKII (Tascam)

## High-end:

VS-2400CD (Roland)

AW2400 (Yamaha)

VS-2480CD (Roland)  DPS24 MKII (Akai)

Compared to stand-alone workstation keyboards and digital audio workstation software, the pros and cons of using a personal digital studio are:

**Pros**: Self-contained and portable. Can go from start to finish (including burning an audio CD). Ability to record non-keyboard sounds (i.e., vocals, horns, etc.) using a microphone. Faders to control the volume levels of each track, which helps when mixing. Learning curve typically faster than for computer-based systems.

**Cons**: Limited to number of tracks available in the machine. Limited editing, mixing, and effects functions compared to computer-based recording systems.

## POP/ROCK

*Pop/rock* is a contemporary music style that uses medium-to-fast tempos, and combines the melodic hooks of pop with the driving energy of rock. Most pop/rock tunes have either a straight-eighths or swing-eighths (shuffle) rhythmic feel. Our first example uses right-hand alternating triads with a straight-eighths rhythmic subdivision, typical of 1980s pop/rock.

TRACK 68

The right-hand triads frequently anticipate beat 1 and then land on the "and" of 1 (leading into beat 2). Meanwhile, the left hand imparts a steady driving feel, with the low root landing on beats 1 and 3, and the root an octave higher landing on beats 2 and 4—the same pattern demonstrated on **Track 51** (p. 70).

## CHORD VOICING TIPS

This example uses alternating triads and upper structures in the right hand as follows:

- Alternating between major triads built from the fifth and the root, on the D chord (adding the seventh and ninth).

- Alternating between major triads built from the seventh and the third, on the Bm7 and Em7 chords (adding the ninth and eleventh).

- Alternating between major triads built from the seventh and the root, on the A11 chords.

- Alternating between major triads built from the fifth, ninth, and root, on the Gmaj7 chord (adding the ninth, sharped eleventh, and thirteenth).

- Alternating between major triads built from the 4th and the root, on the last D chord, and leading into the A chord. (This interior IV-I triad movement is also known as backcycling.)

- The B11 chord is voiced by building a major triad from the seventh: A/B.

 The next example is in a swing-eighths (or *shuffle*) rhythmic style, and uses a mixture of different triads over a repeated bass note (sometimes referred to as a *pedal point*).

TRACK 69

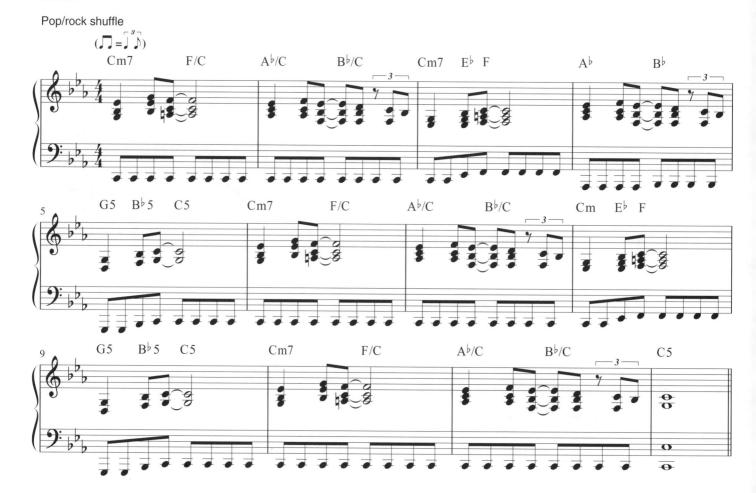

As well as the different triads placed over the same bass note in measures 1–2, 6–7, and 10–11, we have some root-fifth voicings in measures 5, 9, and 12, and some resolving suspensions (fourth moving to third) inside the B♭ triads. The left hand is providing a solid rhythmic pulse, mostly playing the tonic of C, and sometimes moving to other notes in the C minor pentatonic scale (E♭, F, G, B♭). The phrase-lengths are a little unusual here: five, then four, then three measures; see if you can hear this!

### CHORD VOICING TIPS

The different right-hand triads placed over C in the left hand are derived as follows:

- The Cm7 chord is voiced by building a major triad from the third: E♭/C.

- The F/C chord is the result of placing the F chord over its fifth (C) in the bass.

- The A♭/C chord is the result of placing the A♭ chord over its third (C) in the bass. This is embellished with an Fm triad on beat 2 of these measures.

- The B♭/C chord is equivalent to a C11 (major triad built from the seventh). The upper B♭ triad has an interior 4-3 resolution (i.e., E♭ moving to D).

The G5, B♭5, and C5 chords are all voiced with root-fifth intervals in the right hand.

## POSTURE AND POSITION

The key to having good *posture* is to be comfortable, but not to be hunched over or slumped in front of the keyboard. Your back should be fairly straight, and your hands, arms, wrists, and shoulder and back muscles should all be relaxed. You should resist any tendency to lean too far forward, and your feet should be resting on the floor. If you are sitting at the correct height, your hands and forearms should be parallel to the floor, with the fingers touching the keys, as shown:

If you have bad posture (slumped or slouched back, forearms not parallel to floor, too much tension in wrists and/or fingers, etc.), a number of bad things can happen: backache, cramped hands, even carpal tunnel syndrome. So good posture is essential, and will enable you to enjoy playing a whole lot more!

The *position* of the hands and fingers while playing deserves special mention here. You should try to keep your fingers curved and your hands arched as much as you can. You'll build better stamina and technique this way, and have better access to all the keys on the keyboard.

One way to learn this position is to hold a tennis ball in each hand. This way you will naturally arch the hand and curve the fingers, as shown here:

Do not tense up when learning this position; keep the wrist, hand, and fingers as relaxed as possible.

# PRACTICE HABITS

Here are some good tips to help you get the most out of your valuable practice time.

1) **Set goals and priorities for each practice session**. For example, in a half-hour session, you might work for five or more minutes on technique (say, some scales and/or technique exercises), five or more minutes on sightreading (playing some music without having seen it before), and then the remaining time on the tune(s) you are currently learning.

2) **Aim to play the pieces you're working on as smoothly and clearly as possible**. Isolate any rough spots and work on these until you can play them without pausing. For beginners, this will often require finding the correct hand position and fingering.

3) **Play in tempo and slow the piece down as needed**. I sometimes hear beginning-level students rush through pieces too fast, stumble over some notes, then resume playing (too fast again), and so on. This is exactly the WRONG way to go about it (and is also irritating to listen to...)! You should find the tempo at which you are comfortable playing (without any stumbles)—even if the tempo is really slow, it doesn't matter. This will help you play more evenly, as well as help to get the piece into your muscle memory so that your hands begin to learn it; then you can gradually increase the tempo as your facility improves.

4) **Practice pieces with hands separately as needed**. This is very important. Separating the two hands allows you to focus on each hand's part individually. Then, when you re-combine the hands, you'll have a head start, as you'll already be familiar with the individual parts. Actually, in contemporary styles such as blues and rock 'n' roll, the left-hand pattern is often rather repetitive, so practicing this part separately will help you put the left hand on "auto pilot."

5) **Practice with a metronome as needed**. A metronome is a machine (either mechanical or electronic) that emits a steady ticking sound, reminding you of the tempo. Listen hard when playing along, to make sure that you are not slowing down or speeding up. I would suggest that beginning players use a metronome for at least half of each practice session.

6) **Always try to keep going when practicing a performance**. When you see a tune for the first time (unless you're an experienced player!), it's normal to be a little uncertain and make mistakes as you learn it. But once you're familiar with the piece, then the next stage is to practice *performing* it. Do your best to convey the emotion and expressiveness of the music, and above all keep going even if you make a mistake. If there is still some work to do on certain sections of the piece, then isolate and work on them afterwards.

7) **Make sure you are relaxed while practicing**. Maintain proper *posture* and *position*. Don't tense up; make sure your arms, wrists, and fingers are all relaxed. Take a short break every so often to relax; then start up again when you feel refreshed.

8) **Find the right practice environment**. Ideally you should practice in a quiet place, free from interruptions, phones ringing, etc. If your piano or keyboard is in a room where you can close the door, so much the better. Also try to find a time of day when you have some energy and are not too tired.

Good luck with your practicing!

# QUARTER NOTES AND RESTS

A *quarter note* lasts for one beat. This is equivalent to a quarter of a measure in 4/4 time. Here is an example of how quarter notes are written.

The rhythmic counting (1 2 3 4) is shown below the notes in this measure.

The quarter note is written as a black (or filled-in) notehead, with a stem attached.

Next we'll see an example of a quarter rest (which also lasts for one beat).

Here's a notation example that uses some quarter notes and rests.

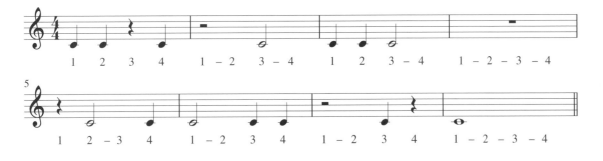

Note that the rhythmic sum of all the notes and rests in each measure agrees with the time signature (i.e., four beats in each 4/4 measure).

For information on other basic rhythmic values, see *Eighth Notes and Rests* (p. 38), *Half Notes and Rests* (p. 56), *Sixteenth Notes and Rests* (p. 104), and *Whole Notes and Rests* (p. 121).

# R&B

*R&B* (rhythm and blues) is an American music style that emerged in the 1950s, and has flourished and developed up until the present day. R&B originally evolved from the jump blues styles made popular in the 1940s, and was an important precursor of the rock 'n' roll styles that emerged in the mid-1950s.

Nowadays the term R&B has come to encompass all black popular music, and therefore includes various sub-categories such as soul, funk, disco, dance-pop, hip-hop, neo-soul, and more. In this section we're going to spotlight two R&B sub-styles: Motown and neo-soul. Motown soul emerged in Detroit in the 1960s, fusing blues, gospel, and pop elements to create a uniquely commercial sound. This up-tempo Motown example has a swing-eighths rhythmic feel.

TRACK 70

This simple rhythmic style anticipates beat 3 by an eighth note in both hands. Upper-structure triads are used in the right hand to create four-part chords, with some arpeggio embellishments beginning in measure 5. The left hand starts by playing the root of each chord, and then switches to root-seventh intervals (a device borrowed from jazz and blues styles) in measure 5.

## CHORD VOICING TIPS

This Motown soul example uses upper-structure triad shapes as follows:

- The Amaj7 and Dmaj7 chords are voiced by building minor triads from the third: C♯m/A and F♯m/D.

- The Bm7 and C♯m7 chords are voiced by building major triads from the third: D/B and E/C♯.

- The E11 chord is voiced by building a major triad from the seventh: D/E.

Our next example is in a neo-soul style. Neo-soul is a twenty-first-century fusion of classic soul (from the 1960s–70s) and contemporary urban/hip-hop production. This example is a ballad, using sixteenth-note rhythmic subdivisions.

TRACK 71

**Neo-soul ballad**

This example has a more open feel at the beginning, with simple root-fifth and root-seventh intervals in the left hand, below the floating 5ths and 6ths of the right hand (as with most ballad styles, be sure to depress the sustain pedal for the duration of each chord). The energy then increases from measure 5 onwards, with sixteenth-note rhythms and anticipations typical of R&B ballads, but with more sophisticated double-4th and cluster chord shapes being used.

## CHORD VOICING TIPS

This neo-soul example uses intervals, upper-structure triads, and double-4th and cluster shapes as follows:

- On the Dm11 chord, the C-G, F-C, and D-A intervals provide the seventh-eleventh, third-seventh, and root-fifth of the chord. (These intervals all come from the D minor pentatonic scale).

- On the B♭6/9 chord, the same C-G, F-C, and D-A intervals provide the ninth-sixth, fifth-ninth, and third-seventh of the chord.

- On the Gm11 chord, the B♭-G, F-C, and D-A intervals provide the third-root, seventh-eleventh, and fifth-ninth of the chord.

- On the C11 chord, the B♭-G, F-C, D-A, C-G, and B♭-F intervals provide the seventh-fifth, eleventh-root, ninth-thirteenth, root-fifth, and seventh-eleventh of the chord.

- The B♭maj7 chord is voiced by building a minor triad from the third: Dm/B♭.

- The Fsus2/A chord is voiced by building a double-4th shape from the ninth (G-C-F).

- The Gm9 chord is voiced with a cluster voicing containing the ninth, third, and fifth (A-B♭-D). (I use the term "cluster" in my books to describe a three-note voicing consisting of a 3rd above a 2nd.)

- The E♭(add9) chord is voiced using a 9-1 resolution within an E♭ major triad.

- The Am7 chord is voiced with a "7-3" voicing (the seventh and third of the chord).

- The Gm7 chord is voiced by building a major triad from the third: B♭/G.

- The A♭sus2 chord is voiced with an inverted double-4th shape built from the ninth (B♭-E♭-A♭), preceded by a cluster voicing containing the root, ninth, and sharped eleventh (A♭-B♭-D).

- The D♭6/9(maj7) chord is voiced by building two double-4th shapes: from the seventh (C-F-B♭) and sixth (B♭-E♭-A♭).

- The C(add9) chord is voiced with an inverted double-4th shape built from the ninth (D-G-C).

## FURTHER READING

For more information on the upper-structure, double-4th, and cluster shapes used in this neo-soul example, please check out my *Contemporary Music Theory: Level Three*, published by Hal Leonard Corporation.

# REPERTOIRE

Most keyboard players need to be concerned with *repertoire* (that is, the quantity of tunes they know). If you're a jazz player, it's desirable to know the established jazz standards (and probably a selection of Latin/Brazilian tunes). On the other hand, if you play in classic rock cover bands, it would be handy to know the famous classic rock anthems from the '60s and '70s. If you aspire to play casual, wedding, or corporate gigs, a good repertoire across a range of styles is an indispensable asset. For tips on committing these songs to memory, see *Memorizing Songs* (p. 74).

As a good starting point for developing your repertoire, here is a list of songs in different styles that I would recommend you become familiar with. Get out those fake books, and start playing!

## JAZZ STANDARDS

| | |
|---|---|
| All the Things You Are | Misty |
| Autumn Leaves | My Romance |
| Body and Soul | Night and Day |
| A Foggy Day | Our Love Is Here to Stay |
| On Green Dolphin Street | Stella by Starlight |

## LATIN & BRAZILIAN

| | |
|---|---|
| Wave | The Girl from Ipanema |
| Desafinado | Triste |
| Black Orpheus | How Insensitive |

### R&B CLASSICS

The Dock of the Bay

In the Midnight Hour

Soul Man

When a Man Loves a Woman

Through the Fire

What's Going On

After the Love Has Gone

Get Ready

### '50s POP

Rock Around the Clock

Love Me Tender

Long Tall Sally

All Shook Up

Blue Suede Shoes

### '60s POP

Surfin' U.S.A.

Hey Jude

Whiter Shade of Pale

Something

Under the Boardwalk

### '70s POP

Imagine

Crocodile Rock

Baker Street

Layla

Dancing Queen

### '80s POP

Every Breath You Take

Sailing

Don't You Forget About Me

Careless Whisper

Candle in the Wind

### '90s POP

Power of Love

Save the Best for Last

Tears in Heaven

Mr. Jones

Losing My Religion

# ROCK 'N' ROLL

*Rock 'n' roll* emerged onto the American music scene in the 1950s, combining elements of the blues, R&B, country, and gospel music at the time, and fusing them in a new way to create a highly rhythmic and danceable style.

A lot of early rock 'n' roll used a straight-eighths rhythmic feel, contrasting with the swing-eighths rhythms common in previous popular styles. Like the blues, a lot of rock 'n' roll tunes use a twelve-measure progression or form consisting of three four-measure phrases, which start with the I, IV, and V chords of the key (chords built from the 1st, 4th, and 5th degrees), respectively. Most piano rock 'n' roll (again like the blues) uses very driving left-hand patterns, as in the following straight-eighths example.

Rock 'n' roll

The right hand is using a mix of patterns derived from the C blues scale and the C and F Mixolydian modes, as well as some chromatically ascending and descending 6ths. The left hand is playing a driving, repetitive root-fifth and root-sixth pattern borrowed from piano blues and boogie styles.

## CHORD VOICING TIPS

This rock 'n' roll example uses blues scales, Mixolydian modes, and patterns in 6ths, as follows:

- On the C7 chord in measures 1 and 11, and the F7 chord in measures 5 and 10, we are using the tonic of the C blues scale (C) as a drone (repeated top note) above the "♭5-5" (F♯-G) underneath.

- On the F7 chord in measures 2 and 6, and the G7 chord in measure 9, we are using the 7th of the C blues scale (B♭) as a drone above the "♭5-5" (F♯-G) underneath.

- On the C7 chord in measures 3, 7, and 11, we are using 3rds from the C Mixolydian mode (G-B♭, F-A, E-G), with some half-step approach tones or grace notes into the third and fifth of the chord.

- On the F7 chord in measure 10, we are using 3rds from the F Mixolydian mode (G-B♭, F-A, E♭-G).

- On the C7 chord in measures 4 and 12, we are using a descending pattern in 6ths (G-E, G♭-E♭, F-D, E-C) to connect the fifth and third of the chord (on beat 1) to the third and root (halfway through beat 2).

- On the C7 chord in measure 8, we are using an ascending pattern in 6ths (G-E, A♭-F, A-F♯, B♭-G) to connect the fifth and third of the chord (on beat 1) to the seventh and fifth (again halfway through beat 2).

Next we will look at a rock 'n' roll shuffle (swing-eighths) pattern. As we have seen, the swing-eighths rhythmic subdivision typically uses the first and third parts of the (implied) eighth-note triplet for each beat. However, in swing-eighths blues and rock 'n' roll styles we also have the option to use all three parts of the triplet, as shown in the following example.

TRACK 73

This time the right hand is using 3rds and triads from the C and F Mixolydian modes, as well as some four-part upper structures for the busier eighth-note triplets.

## CHORD VOICING TIPS

This rock 'n' roll shuffle example uses blues scales, Mixolydian modes and triads, upper-structure four-part chord shapes, and 6th patterns in the right hand, as follows:

- On the C7 chord in measures 1, 3, and 11, we are using 3rds from the C Mixolydian mode (G-B♭, F-A, E-G), with some half-step approach tones or grace notes into the third and fifth of the chord.

- On the F7 chord in measure 2, we are using 3rds from the F Mixolydian mode (G-B♭, F-A, E♭-G), with some half-step approach tones or grace notes into the seventh and ninth of the chord.

- The F7 chords in measures 5 and 10, the C7 chord in measure 7, and the G7 chord in measure 9 are all voiced (on beats 1–3) by building minor-seventh-flatted-fifth four-part shapes from the third: Am7♭5/F, Em7♭5/C, and Bm7♭5/G. These voicings upgrade all the chords to dominant ninths.

- On the F7 chord at the end of measure 5 leading into measure 6, and at the end of measure 10, we are using second-inversion triads from the F Mixolydian mode (Cm, B♭, Adim, Gm, F), with some half-step approach tones into the third of the chord. Similarly at the end of measure 9, the Bdim triad is derived from G Mixolydian.

- On the C7 chord at the end of measure 7 leading into measure 8, we are using second-inversion triads from the C Mixolydian mode (F, Edim, Dm, C), again with some half-step approach tones into the third of the chord.

- Elsewhere we are using embellishments from the C blues scale (at the end of measures 4 and 8) and patterns of descending 6ths (at the end of measure 3, and at the end of measure 11 leading into measure 12).

The left hand is using the same root-fifth and root-sixth pattern as in the previous example (adapted for the shuffle rhythm), with a chromatic walkup into the ending in measure 12.

## FURTHER READING

For more info on rock 'n' roll and blues piano styles, please check out my *Blues Piano: The Complete Guide with CD!*, published by Hal Leonard Corporation.

# SEQUENCER

A *sequencer* is a software program or hardware device that facilitates multitrack recording and playback. The first sequencers (in the 1980s) were essentially MIDI data recorders. Software sequencers (running on a Mac or PC) started out as MIDI-only, and then added digital audio capability in the 1990s (with the arrival of faster computers) to become digital audio workstations. Hardware sequencers (which could be used in live performance) also started out using MIDI data, and then added digital audio and sampling in the 1990s.

Modern hardware sequencers are stand-alone devices, typically with drum pads to facilitate the recording of drum and percussion parts. These are often referred to as "sampling groove workstations." Probably the most notable piece of equipment in this category is the Akai MPC60, which was instrumental in shaping today's hip-hop styles. Workstation keyboards usually contain on-board sequencers, and may also have sampling capability.

Arranger keyboards also generally offer sequencing capability. These are functionally similar to workstation keyboards, but are primarily for the home market and for hobbyists (as opposed to workstation keyboards, which are used in live performance). Arranger keyboards normally have built-in speakers, on-board rhythm patterns, and automatic accompaniment features.

For summaries of leading equipment, see *Digital Audio Workstation* (p. 32) and *Workstation Keyboard* (p. 123). Here are some examples of other devices with sequencing capability in 2007.

### Hardware sequencers/sampling groove workstations

MPC500, MPC1000, MPC2500 (Akai)

MC-808, MV-8800 (Roland)

Electribe Series (Korg)

Akai MPC500

### Arranger keyboards

PSR1500, PSR3000, Tyros2 (Yamaha)

E-09, G-70 (Roland)

PA800, PA1X ProElite (Korg)

Korg PA800

# SEVENTH CHORDS

*Seventh chords* are four-part chords in which the highest extension is the seventh (the note that is a 7th above the root). Most four-part chords will have a seventh, although some will have a sixth instead. Here is a summary of the seventh chords found commonly in contemporary styles, with the addition of the widely used major sixth chord (which has a sixth instead of a seventh).

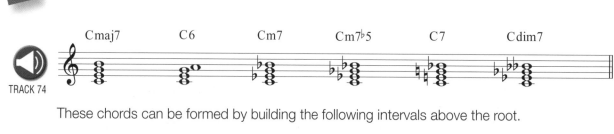

TRACK 74

These chords can be formed by building the following intervals above the root.

| | |
|---|---|
| major seventh chord: | major 3rd, perfect 5th, major 7th (1-3-5-7) |
| major sixth chord: | major 3rd, perfect 5th, major 6th (1-3-5-6) |
| minor seventh chord: | minor 3rd, perfect 5th, minor 7th (1-♭3-5-♭7). |
| minor seventh-flatted fifth chord: | minor 3rd, diminished 5th, minor 7th (1-♭3-♭5-♭7) |
| dominant seventh chord: | major 3rd, perfect 5th, minor 7th (1-3-5-♭7) |
| diminished seventh chord: | minor 3rd, diminished 5th, diminished 7th (1-♭3-♭5-♭♭7) |

Note that most of these chord qualities are found within a major scale, as diatonic seventh chords.

# SIXTEENTH NOTES AND RESTS

A *sixteenth note* lasts for a quarter of a beat. This is equivalent to a sixteenth of a measure in 4/4 time. Here is an example of some different ways that sixteenth notes can be written.

The rhythmic counting (1 e & a 2 e & a 3 e & a 4 e & a, etc.) is shown below the notes in this measure. The "e" and "a" subdivisions fall in between the eighth-note subdivisions.

The sixteenth note is written as a black (or filled-in) notehead, with a stem attached, and either two flags if the note is by itself (like the first four notes in the above example) or two beams if the note is joined to other notes (as in the remaining notes above). Sometimes the beams may join two sixteenth notes together within half a beat (as in the first two beamed pairs above), or the beams may join all of the sixteenth notes within one beat (as in the last two beats above).

Next we'll see an example of a sixteenth rest (which also lasts for a quarter of a beat).

Here's a notation example that combines some sixteenth notes and rests.

Note that the rhythmic sum of all the notes and rests in each measure agrees with the time signature (i.e., four beats for each 4/4 measure).

For information on other basic rhythmic values, see *Eighth Notes and Rests* (p. 38), *Quarter Notes and Rests* (p. 95), *Half Notes and Rests* (p. 56), and *Whole Notes and Rests* (p. 121).

## SOLOING

*Soloing* normally involves improvising a single-note melodic line over a chord progression. There are various techniques available to you when soloing over chord changes, including arpeggios, neighbor tones, and target notes. Another very useful technique when soloing is to use different scales, either on a chord-by-chord basis, or determined by the key of the song. In practice, these soloing techniques can be freely mixed (for example, you might use scale tones to connect between target notes). In this section we'll look at some soloing examples using scales, beginning with the following country/rock example.

TRACK 75

Country/rock

This solo uses pentatonic scales built from the roots of the major chords, and from the thirds of the minor chords. For example, over the G major chords we are using notes from the G pentatonic scale (G-A-B-D-E), and over the A minor chords we are using notes from the C pentatonic scale (C-D-E-G-A), which is equivalent to the A minor pentatonic scale. Changing scales on a chord-by-chord basis like this is referred to as "playing *through* the changes" (and will make your solo sound more "inside" the chords).

The simple patterns in the first half of the above example are a good starting point for your own pentatonic improvisations. Notice that even if you just move up and down the pentatonic scale, the results will typically sound melodic and useful (this is due to the sequence of minor 3rds and whole steps in the scale). The second half of the example has some busier sixteenth-note figures, which are four-note pentatonic groups—like those in the scale exercise on **Track 33** (p. 42). This type of figure is useful across a range of pop and rock styles.

In simple contemporary styles, the solo typically lands on a chord tone at the points of chord change (beat 1 of each measure in this case). In this example, the solo plays the root of the chord on beat 1 of measures 1 and 2, the 3rd of the chord on beat 1 of measures 3 and 4, and so on. These chord tones might also be target notes used as a framework around which the solo is developed.

Our next example is a more sophisticated jazz/blues, and uses the blues scale as a source of notes for the solo.

Jazz/blues

This solo uses the blues scale built from the tonic of the key (the A blues scale in this case), playing it over all the chords in this twelve-bar blues progression. This is referred to as "playing over the changes" (using one scale over the whole chord progression, rather than changing scales on a chord-by-chord basis). Some vertical dissonances may occur when doing this, but the character and linear strength of the blues scale normally makes the ear forgive these contradictions. Use this example as a springboard for your own blues solo ideas!

### FURTHER READING

For more information on creating solos in jazz styles, please check out my *Smooth Jazz Piano: The Complete Guide with CD!* and *Jazz-Blues Piano: The Complete Guide with CD!*, both published by Hal Leonard Corporation.

## STACCATO

To play *staccato* means to play the notes in a short and separated style (as opposed to legato). *Staccato* playing is often needed in today's rock and funk styles, as shown in the following straight-eighths rock example.

Rock

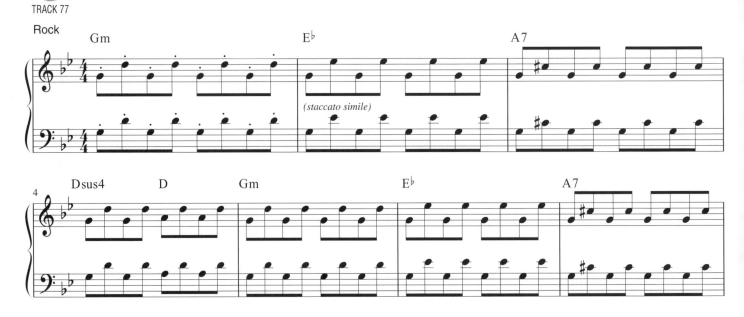

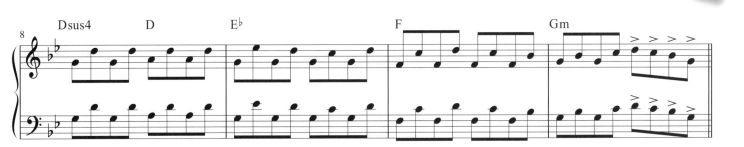

In this *staccato* rock style, the two hands are playing the same notes an octave apart, alternating between two chord tones on each chord. For example, on the Gm chord the root is alternating with the fifth, on the E♭ chord the third is alternating with the root, and so on. These chord tones are chosen to voice lead from left to right, to avoid unnecessary interval skips between chords. Starting in measure 9 the top note is varied to create some melodic interest, leading to an ending riff derived from the G minor pentatonic scale.

## SUSPENDED CHORDS

A *suspended chord* is a chord in which the third has been replaced by another note, most often the fourth (the note that is a perfect 4th above the root). In mainstream styles, suspensions can be applied to triads (normally major), or seventh chords (normally dominant sevenths). Within a triad, the second (or ninth) can also replace the third of the chord. The following example shows suspensions applied to a C triad (first measure) and a C7 chord (second measure).

We can compare these suspensions to the original chords as follows:

- If we replace the third of the C major triad with the second (D is a major 2nd above C), we get the Csus2 chord.

- If we replace the third of the C major triad with the fourth (F is a perfect 4th above C), we get the Csus4 chord (if you see the symbol "Csus," then Csus4 is assumed).

- If we replace the third of the C7 chord with the fourth (F is a perfect 4th above C), we get the C7sus4 chord (if you see the symbol "C7sus," then C7sus4 is assumed).

We'll now make use of these triad and four-part sus4 chords in a style example. First, here are the chords we're going to use.

TRACK 78
Part 1

Now we arpeggiate and split these chords in various ways, creating a slow sixteenth-note rock groove.

Slow rock

In the first four measures the suspended triads are arpeggiated, starting with the left hand and continuing with the right. In the second four measures the suspended dominant seventh chords are split into 4ths and 5ths, over a root-to-fifth pattern in the left hand. Here the sixteenth-note rhythmic conversation between the hands is reminiscent of funk styles, but with more sustain and legato phrasing used.

## SUSTAIN PEDAL

The *sustain* (or *damper*) *pedal* lifts all the dampers off the strings, enabling them to continue vibrating after the keys are released. On digital pianos and synthesizers, this effect is re-created electronically. Pedals for electronic instruments come in a variety of models, with two basic styles, one that is similar to the pedal on an acoustic piano, and another that is more of a plain small box (see photos below). On most digital pianos, the pedal is attached to the instrument, whereas with other keyboards and synthesizers, the pedal is something extra that gets plugged into a jack on the back (or sometimes the side) of the keyboard.

In contemporary music, the use of the pedal is very style-dependent. For example, it is very common to use the pedal in ballad styles, so that the notes from each chord all sound together (before the pedal is released at the point of chord change). However, the pedal is used sparingly (if at all) in more up-tempo rock and funk styles, as it will detract from the rhythmic drive and/or syncopations used.

Here is a simple pop ballad comping example to demonstrate the use of the sustain pedal. The open-triad patterns in the left hand require the sustain pedal to be used for the duration of each chord. On the CD track, this example is first played without the sustain pedal; you can hear that it sounds rather dry and spare. The second time, however, the sustain pedal is added, allowing the notes of the left-hand arpeggios to blend together within each chord, creating a fuller effect.

TRACK 79

Pop ballad

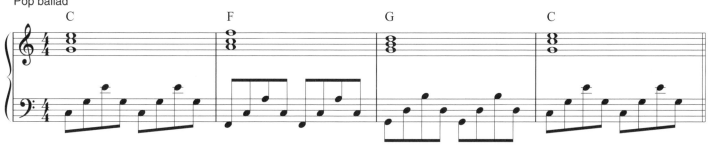

In this example the right hand is playing whole-note inverted triads, with voice leading.

# TARGET NOTES

A *target note* is a note within a chord that is a desirable "landing point" for a solo (or melody) played over that chord. A series of target notes, therefore, gives us a framework around which a solo can be developed. In more basic contemporary styles, a target note might be just the root, third, or fifth of a triad. In styles using extended chords (i.e., jazz and R&B), target notes can be expanded to include sevenths, ninths, elevenths, and/or thirteenths. Also, in jazz styles we might make use of altered fifths and/or ninths, as these have a lot of color and character.

In practice, when soloing we might combine target notes with other techniques, such as arpeggios, neighbor tones, and the use of scales such as pentatonic or blues.

The first half of each solo in this section contains only the target notes to be used over each chord. Then in the second half of each example, we repeat the chord progression, creating a solo around the framework of these target notes. Our first example uses chord thirds and sevenths as target notes (a jazz staple), and is in a smooth jazz/funk style.

TRACK 80

Smooth jazz/funk

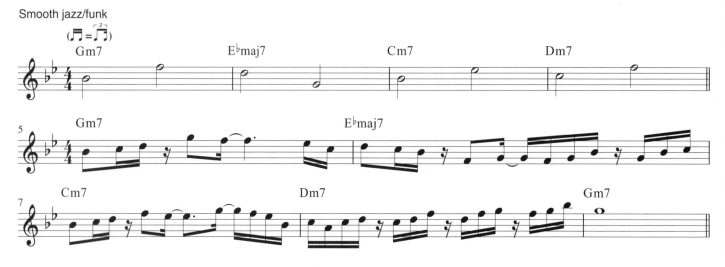

In the first measure, the target notes are B♭ and F (the third and seventh of the Gm7 chord), followed in the second measure by D and G (the seventh and third of the E♭maj7 chord), and so on. These target notes also occur in the solo over the last four measures, now with added connecting tones and rhythms in between. In this case the added notes are from the B♭ and F pentatonic scales. The rhythms are typical of funk and smooth jazz styles, with sixteenth-note subdivisions and anticipations.

The next example is in a more sophisticated jazz vein, and uses the flatted thirteenth (equivalent to the sharped fifth) as a target note on some dominant chords. Again we see just the target notes in the first half, and the full solo over the same chord changes in the second half.

TRACK 81

Jazz swing

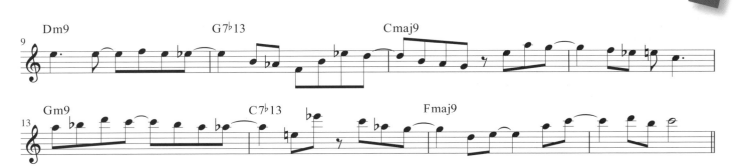

Note that this solo example consists of two II-V-I progressions (chords built from the 2nd, 5th, and 1st degrees of a key—the two keys here being C major, then F major), which is a cornerstone of jazz harmony. The target notes over both keys create a "9-♭13-9" line over this progression: in measures 1–3 the target notes are E (the ninth of the Dm9 chord), E♭ (the flatted thirteenth of the G7♭13 chord), and D (the ninth of the Cmaj9 chord). The added notes in between the target notes are a mix of neighbor tones, arpeggiated chord tones, and pentatonic scales. Note the resulting solo phrases often start and/or end on an upbeat, which is common in mainstream jazz and blues styles.

### FURTHER READING

For more information on using target notes to create solos and melodies in jazz styles, please check out my *Smooth Jazz Piano: The Complete Guide with CD!* and *Jazz-Blues Piano: The Complete Guide with CD!*, both published by Hal Leonard Corporation.

# THUMB TURN

A *thumb turn* occurs when the thumb passes underneath the other fingers, or when the other fingers pass over the thumb. This normally happens when playing scales, arpeggios, or crossovers licks.

Let's see how thumb turns would be used when playing the C major scale. Fingering is shown for both hands.

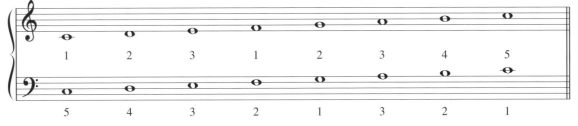

When playing the above scale with the right hand:

    1) **Ascending**    After playing E with the third finger, the thumb passes under the fingers to play F.

    2) **Descending**    After playing F with the thumb, the fingers pass over the thumb so that the third finger can play F.

When playing the above scale with the left hand:

    1) **Ascending**    After playing G with the thumb, the fingers pass over the thumb so that the third finger can play A.

    2) **Descending**    After playing A with the third finger, the thumb passes under the fingers to play G.

Always strive to keep the thumb mobile when executing these thumb turns: look ahead and move the thumb smoothly to its destination as soon as possible.

## TIED NOTES

*Tied notes* are connected by a curved line in the music, indicating that the first note is to be played and then held for the combined duration of all the tied notes. The tie connects two or more notes of the same pitch. Here is an example incorporating tied notes.

The most common reason for using a tie is to extend a note's duration beyond the barline. In the first measure above, the only way to have a note landing on beat 4 last for two beats is to have a quarter note tied to another quarter note in the next measure. (If we wrote a half note starting on beat 4, we would have too many beats for a 4/4 measure.)

Another reason for using a tie is to show the start of beat 3 in a 4/4 measure, as a courtesy to musicians who are sightreading the music. In the first measure of the above example, the eighth note landing on the "and" of 2 is tied to the following quarter note. Technically we could have written a dotted quarter note, but this would have hidden beat 3 from view. Having the primary beats (1 and 3 in 4/4) visible is helpful, particularly if the music is being read at a fast tempo.

If your music contains sixteenth notes, it's considered good form to show the start of each beat (i.e., beats 2 and 4 as well as 1 and 3); again, using ties will help you do this. If you're writing music to be read by other players, they will thank you for it!

## TRIADS

A *triad* is a three-note chord, consisting of a root, third, and fifth. There are four triads in common usage: major, minor, augmented, and diminished.

TRACK 82

These chords can be formed by building the following *intervals* above the root.

| | |
|---|---|
| major triad: | major 3rd, perfect 5th (1-3-5) |
| minor triad: | minor 3rd, perfect 5th (1-♭3-5) |
| augmented triad: | major 3rd, augmented 5th (1-3-♯5) |
| diminished triad: | minor 3rd, diminished 5th (1-♭3-♭5) |

Note that most of these triad qualities are found within a major scale, as diatonic triads.

# UPBEATS

An *upbeat* falls in between the beats (i.e., halfway through beat 1, 2, 3, or 4 in a 4/4 measure)—as opposed to a downbeat, which falls on the beat. This is illustrated as follows.

When we count eighth-note rhythms this way (1 & 2 &, etc.), we can see that the downbeats fall on 1, 2, 3, and 4, and the upbeats fall on the &s in between (referred to as the "and-of-1," "and-of-2," etc.).

TRACK 83

Jazz swing styles often emphasize upbeats, as shown in the following comping example.

This more sophisticated jazz example uses polychord (chord-over-chord) voicings, similar to the jazz/blues example on **Track 47** (p. 64). Apart from the chords played on beat 1 of measures 1, 3, 5, and 7, note that all the other voicings land on upbeats, creating a syncopated effect that is common in mainstream jazz styles.

## CHORD VOICING TIPS

This jazz swing example uses triads (with octave doubling) in the right hand, over double-4th shapes in the left hand. Double 4ths here include shapes with a diminished 4th (equal to a major 3rd) interval on top.

- The Em11 chord is voiced by building a major triad from the third in the right hand, over a double-4th shape (eleventh-seventh-third) built from the eleventh in the left hand.

- The A7($\sharp$5,$\sharp$9) chord is voiced by building a major triad from the sharped fifth in the right hand, over a double-4th shape (seventh-third-sharped fifth) built from the seventh in the left hand.

- The A7($\flat$5,$\flat$9) chord is voiced by building a major triad from the flatted fifth in the right hand, over the same double-4th shape (seventh-third-sharped fifth) built from the seventh in the left hand.

- The D6/9(maj7) chord is voiced with various triads in the right hand: major triads built from the root and fifth, and a minor triad built from the sixth. These are all placed over a double-4th shape (third-sixth-ninth) built from the third in the left hand.

- The Am11 chord is voiced by building a major triad from the third in the right hand, over a double-4th shape (root-eleventh-seventh) built from the root in the left hand.

- The D9 chord is voiced by building a major triad from the root and a minor triad from the fifth in the right hand, over a double-4th shape (third-seventh-ninth) built from the third in the left hand.

- The G6/9(maj7) chord is voiced by building minor triads from the third and sixth in the right hand, over a double-4th shape (sixth-ninth-fifth) built from the sixth in the left hand.

## UPGRADING CHORDS

If you are faking a keyboard part, either working from a chart or from memory, some chord upgrading may be desirable. This means taking basic chord symbols (for example, triads) and adding upper extensions and/or alterations. The triad, seventh-chord, and double-4th upper-structure voicings we have used in this book offer a convenient and suitable way to upgrade chords in contemporary styles. In simpler pop/rock/R&B applications, we're unlikely to alter the chord (meaning flat or sharp the fifth and/or ninth by half step), and any extensions added (seventh, ninth, eleventh, thirteenth) will most often be diatonic (i.e., within the key of the song). By contrast, jazz musicians routinely add extensions and alterations to basic chord symbols—when playing a chart from a fake book, for example.

In this section we'll take a simple rock progression with basic triad chord symbols, and then upgrade these chords using upper-structure triad voicings. This will not only add extensions to the chords, but also impart that triad-over-root sound that is so appropriate for contemporary pop styles. Our starting point is a basic pop/rock groove using simple triads, as reflected in the chord symbols.

TRACK 84

Note that the right-hand voicings exactly match the chord symbols—no chord upgrading has occurred. We are still voice leading the triads from left to right, and anticipating beat 1 of each even-numbered measure by an eighth note—both standard pop/rock techniques. This would work fine for a simple song. But in the next version, we have upgraded the chords by using upper-structure triads, creating a more sophisticated sound.

TRACK 85

To help you to understand better how the chords have been upgraded, the chord symbols for version 2 have been changed to reflect the extensions added. However, in practice the experienced player would apply this upgrading in real time, working from the basic chord symbols shown for version 1. Here's how the chords were upgraded with upper-structure triads.

- On the minor chords Cm and Fm, we built major triads from the thirds: E♭/C and A♭/F, which upgraded the chords to minor sevenths. This upgrade of minor chords will work across a wide variety of pop styles (from the Beatles up until the present day).

- On the major chords E♭ and A♭, we built major triads from the fifths: B♭/E♭ and E♭/A♭, which upgraded the chords to major ninths (with the thirds omitted). This upgrade gives the major chord a bright and transparent sound, and is good for pop/rock, as well as contemporary jazz styles (in use from around the mid-1970s onwards).

- On the B♭ major chords, we built a major triad from the seventh (which is not even present in the original chord symbol): A♭/B♭. Note that this not a voicing for a major chord; instead we have created a suspended dominant chord (equivalent to a B♭11). In pop and rock songs, this chord quality often occurs on the 5th degree of a major key, and on the 7th degree of a minor key. In this case, the example is in C minor, of which B♭ is the 7th degree. So we took some liberties here by changing the chord from major to suspended dominant. You would not routinely do this in response to a "B♭" chord symbol, of course—but (melody and style permitting) it's a cool sound to drop in occasionally!

# USED EQUIPMENT

In this section we'll cover some basic points about buying and selling musical equipment. Buying used equipment can make sense if you are looking for something that is not manufactured anymore, or if you are trying to save money in comparison to the cost of a new item. Selling used equipment typically occurs if you have something that you no longer need (because you've now upgraded to something better), or if you otherwise need to turn some equipment into money!

The main channels open to you for buying and selling equipment are:

**Online**: In addition to the familiar ebay.com, there are other online classified ad sites (such as recycler.com), as well as dedicated musician sites (such as harmony-central.com). A lot of the equipment items on harmony-central.com are sold to out-of-state customers. So if you're selling, it's advisable to quote a price including shipping. And remember to insure the item(s) for the correct value when shipping.

**Print ads**: Check local papers and classified-ad papers (such as *Recycler*) in your area. In the western U.S. we have *Music Connection* magazine, which contains classified ads for equipment (and is a useful resource in general).

**Stores**: Music stores will often sell used equipment, including floor models or demo items. Check your local music dealer to find good deals.

**Friends**: Buying and selling equipment from/to friends and bandmates is another way to go. You are perhaps more likely to be confident about the item's history and reliability if you buy it from someone you know!

Here are some other things to be aware of if you are buying used equipment.

1) There are normally no warranties available on used equipment (unless you buy from a store), so do your best to evaluate the item(s) beforehand! If you know someone who's a gear expert, consider asking him or her to check the item(s) with you, provided that the seller is in your area.

2) If you are not a technical person, there are still things that you can check for (assuming you're able to try before you buy). If you're buying a keyboard, make sure it produces sound, and that you can activate the basic modes and functions. In the case of an amp, make sure that it produces sound when you plug your keyboard into it, without any noise or distortion (which could indicate problems with the amp and/or speaker). Do a visual check: make sure there are no missing or damaged keys, knobs, switches, etc. Above all, make sure that you like the sound that you're getting; if not, you should say: "No thanks!" Also, ask for any available original packaging; this can help when you are transporting the item (and it looks good if you end up re-selling it).

3) Be aware of the typical price range for the used equipment that you're interested in (by checking websites, publications, etc.). If you're being asked a top price for an item, make sure it's in excellent condition. With the exception of specialty and rare items, it's still generally a buyer's market out there, so feel free to make an offer below the asking price, especially if it's a cash sale!

# VOICE LEADING

*Voice leading* occurs when some of the voicings in a chord progression are inverted, to ensure smooth movement between chords (i.e., movement without large interval skips). Most contemporary styles use voice leading to some degree. In this section we'll see two examples of a progression using basic triads, to be played in a pop ballad style. In the first example, the triads are just voiced in root position (i.e., no inversions or voice leading); you can hear that the motion from one chord to the next sounds rather disconnected. By contrast, the second example uses inversions to connect more smoothly between successive chords.

Each example contains four measures in which the chords are written as whole notes, followed by four measures of comping in a simple pop ballad style. In the comping pattern, the right hand is playing the triads as arpeggios, and the left hand is playing the root of each chord on beats 1 and 3, with an eighth-note pickup into beat 3. Here is the first example, with all the triads in root position.

TRACK 86

Now here's the second example, using triad inversions to voice lead between chords.

TRACK 87

Note that the G triad in measure 2 is in second inversion, to voice lead more closely from the preceding root-position D triad. Similarly, the A triad in measure 3 is in first inversion to voice lead from the preceding G triad. This simple idea will make your comping sound much more musical!

# VOICING

A *voicing* is an interpretation of a chord symbol by the pianist. At a simple level, this could be a decision on how to invert a chord, or how to distribute the notes between the hands. In a more advanced situation, this might involve upgrading a chord symbol by adding extensions and/or using upper structures appropriate for the style.

In this section we'll spotlight minor triads and minor seventh chords, and some of the upper-structure voicings available for them, as well as polychords (chord-over-chord voicings) where each hand is playing a chord shape. As a general rule, using a single upper structure over a root note is more typical in contemporary pop and R&B styles, whereas polychords are normally reserved for jazz applications. Here are some upper structure and polychord voicings available on a C minor chord.

TRACK 88

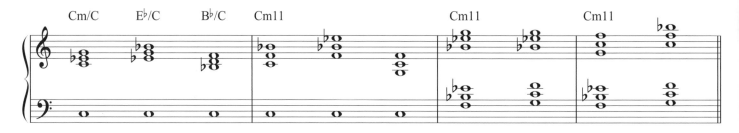

In the first measure, we have some triad-over-root upper-structure voicings. These are upper triads built from some part of the chord.

- The first voicing is a minor triad built from the root (Cm/C).

- The second voicing is a major triad built from the third (E♭/C), creating a minor seventh chord.

- The third voicing is a major triad built from the seventh (B♭/C), creating a less definitive minor eleventh chord (with the third and fifth omitted). In contemporary styles this voicing might alternate with the E♭/C above. This voicing also works for a suspended dominant ninth (a.k.a. dominant eleventh) chord.

In the second measure, we have some double-4th-over-root upper-structure voicings. These are upper double-4th shapes (consisting of two perfect 4ths stacked on top of one another) built from some part of the chord.

- The first voicing is a double 4th built from the root (C-F-B♭), giving us the root, eleventh, and seventh of the chord.

- The second voicing is a double 4th built from the eleventh (F-B♭-E♭), giving us the eleventh, seventh, and third of the chord.

- The third voicing is a double 4th built from the fifth (G-C-F), giving us the fifth, root, and eleventh of the chord.

In the third measure, we have some polychord voicings using triads in the right hand over double 4ths in the left hand. This is a classic jazz sound, pioneered by the legendary pianist Bill Evans in the 1950s. These voicings are sometimes referred to as "rootless," as the left hand is no longer playing the root on the bottom. These voicings use the major triad built from the third of the chord (E♭) in the right hand, over double 4ths built from the eleventh and from the fifth in the left hand. There are several possible combinations, of course!

In the last measure we have some more polychord voicings, with both hands now playing one of the above double-4th shapes, creating a very transparent quality. These are signature sounds in more contemporary and modal jazz styles.

Next we'll put all these voicings to work in some style settings, beginning with an R&B/funk groove using a twelve-bar minor blues progression.

R&B/funk

Here the sixteenth-note subdivisions and anticipations, with the rhythmic interplay between the hands, are typical of funk keyboard styles. The right-hand voicings are a mix of triad and double-4th upper structures.

## CHORD VOICING TIPS

In this R&B/funk example the right hand is using upper-structure triads and double-4th shapes as follows:

- On the Em7 chords, we are alternating between major triads built from the third (G/E) and seventh (D/E), and between double-4th shapes built from the root (E-A-D), eleventh (A-D-G), and fifth (B-E-A).

- On the Am7 chords, we are alternating between major triads built from the third (C/A) and seventh (G/A), and between double-4th shapes built from the eleventh (D-G-C) and fifth (E-A-D).

- On the Bm7 chords, we are alternating between major triads built from the third (D/B) and seventh (A/B), and between double-4th shapes built from the eleventh (E-A-D) and fifth (F♯-B-E).

TRACK 90 The next example is in a modern jazz waltz style, and is typical of the more transparent modal jazz that emerged in the 1960s.

The use of upbeats is similar to that in other jazz swing examples in this book, but adapted here to work in 3/4 time. For example, typical rhythmic figures land on the "and" of 1 and on beat 3 (measures 5 and 13), or on beat 1 and on the "and" of 2 (left hand in measures 7 and 15). The voicings are all polychords.

## CHORD VOICING TIPS

This jazz waltz example uses double 4ths in the left hand, and triads and double 4ths in the right hand, as follows:

- The Bm11 chords are voiced with the following right-hand shapes: a major triad built from the third (D), and double 4ths built from the fifth (F♯-B-E) and from the root (B-E-A). These are placed over double-4th shapes built from the eleventh (E-A-D) and from the fifth (F♯-B-E) in the left hand.

- The Dm11 chords are voiced with the following right-hand shapes: a major triad built from the third (F), and double 4ths built from the fifth (A-D-G) and from the root (D-G-C). These are placed over double-4th shapes built from the eleventh (G-C-F) and from the fifth (A-D-G) in the left hand.

## FURTHER READING

For much more information on chord voicings, polychords, and how to voice all types of chords using upper-structure triads and double-4th shapes, please check out my book *Contemporary Music Theory: Level Three*, published by Hal Leonard Corporation.

# WHOLE NOTES AND RESTS

A *whole note* lasts for four beats. This is equivalent to a whole measure in 4/4 time. Here is an example of how a whole note is written.

The rhythmic counting (1 2 3 4) is shown below the note in this measure.

The whole note is written as a white (or empty) notehead, with no stem attached.

Next we'll see an example of a whole rest (which also lasts for four beats).

Here's a notation example that uses a whole note and a whole note rest.

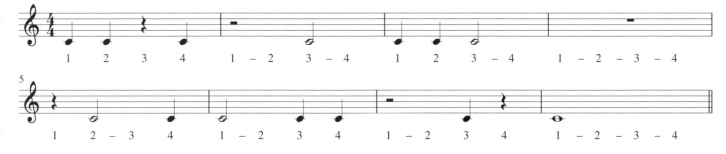

Note that the rhythmic sum of all the notes and rests in each measure agrees with the time signature (i.e., four beats in each 4/4 measure).

For information on other basic rhythmic values, see *Eighth Notes and Rests* (p. 38), *Half Notes and Rests* (p. 56), *Quarter Notes and Rests* (p. 95), and *Sixteenth Notes and Rests* (p. 104).

# WHOLE STEP

The *whole step* is an interval double the size of the half step. If we move from any note on the keyboard to the nearest note on the right or left, and then again in the same direction to the next nearest note, this movement is a whole step. Here are some examples of whole steps.

Whole steps may occur between white keys and/or black keys as follows:

- The whole step C-D is between two white keys.
- The whole step E-F♯ is between a white key and a black key.
- The whole step G♯-A♯ is between two black keys.
- The whole step B♭-C is between a black key and a white key.

Whole steps and half steps are the most common building blocks used when creating scales. Another important relationship to know is that there are six whole steps per octave.

# WHOLE-TONE SCALE

The *whole-tone scale* is a six-note scale that is built using consecutive whole steps. Here is an example of a G whole tone scale.

This scale has a uniquely "floating" and non-definitive character. Note that if we started the above scale on A, it would become an A whole-tone scale, but would contain the same notes; since the scale contains only whole steps, it can be named after any note within the scale. This means there are really only two whole-tone scales in existence: the above scale, and the whole-tone scale created from the six notes absent from the above scale (A♭-B♭-C-D-E-G♭).

In some contemporary situations we may use the whole-tone scale for embellishment over a dominant chord. The above scale contains the root (G), third (B), and seventh (F) of a G7 chord, which are the critical tones of the chord. If we use this scale over a G7 chord, we will also get the ninth (A), flatted fifth (D♭), and sharped fifth (E♭). Here is a mid-tempo pop/R&B groove, in the style of Stevie Wonder, that demonstrates this concept.

Note the G9(♭5,♯5) chord symbols; these have been upgraded (from the basic G7) to reflect the extensions added from the G whole-tone scale. The scale has been used in measures 3–4 and 7–8 in an ascending and descending pattern in 3rds. The left hand is playing a root-fifth-third open-triad pattern on the major chords, and a root-seventh-third pattern on the dominant chords.

## CHORD VOICING TIPS

This pop/R&B example uses an upper-structure four-part chord shape as follows:

- The Cmaj9 chords are voiced by building minor-seventh four-part shapes from the third: Em7/C.

# WORKSTATION KEYBOARD

A *workstation keyboard* is a self-contained keyboard/synthesizer, offering a range of different sounds (pianos, strings, brass, organ, bass, drums, etc.) and on-board sequencing/recording capability. You can go into the sequencer mode on the machine, record the piano part for your song (say on track 1) using one of the on-board sounds, and then go back and record a bass sound on track 2, drums on track 3, and so on, up to the limit of the number of tracks available in the unit (and the number of simultaneous notes that the unit will provide). Although the sound quality on these workstation keyboards is pretty good (and getting better all the time), it will generally not be quite as good as a computer-based recording solution (using a digital audio workstation), due to limitations in computer processing power and memory size.

*Arranger keyboards* are another category of electronic keyboard, which have a lot of the same functions as workstation keyboards, but are more oriented towards the home market and beginners/hobbyists. These machines have built-in speakers, as opposed to workstation keyboards that normally require external amplification. See *Sequencer* (p. 103) for more information on arranger keyboards.

Popular examples of workstation keyboards in 2007 (manufacturers in parentheses) are:

| | | |
|---|---|---|
| **Budget**: | TR Series (Korg) | |
| | Juno-G (Roland) | |
| | GW-7 (Roland) | |

Juno G (Roland)

| | |
|---|---|
| **Mid-range**: | M3 Series (Korg) |
| | Fantom Series (Roland) |
| | Motif Series (Yamaha) |
| | Fusion (Alesis) |
| | K2661 (Kurzweil) |

Fusion (Alesis)

| | |
|---|---|
| **High-end**: | OASYS (Korg) |
| | K2600X (Kurzweil) |

K2600X (Kurzweil)

Compared to personal digital studios and digital audio workstation software, the pros and cons of using a workstation keyboard are as follows:

**Pros**: Completely self-contained: nothing to hook up, no cables, etc. Can go from start to finish (including burning an audio CD) on one piece of equipment. Learning curve typically faster than for computer-based systems.

**Cons**: Limited to the sounds, number of tracks, and number of simultaneous notes available in the machine. Limited editing functions and screen size compared to computer-based recording systems.

# X-RAY YOUR PLAYING

You should always take time to evaluate your playing critically—to "x-ray" it—by recording it and then listening afterwards. You can learn a lot this way—things that might not have been apparent otherwise! Here are a few ways you can do this.

1) **Record yourself while practicing.**

   You can do this while playing an acoustic or electric keyboard, and you can record with a portable digital recorder, or a good old-fashioned cassette machine or boombox! Listen to your performance. Are you stumbling, or are you comfortable with the part? Are you rhythmically consistent? Are you articulating cleanly? Are you projecting the melody properly? Are you using dynamics correctly? And so on....

2) **Record yourself into a sequencer or digital audio workstation.**

   All computer-based sequencers (or digital audio workstations) enable you to "view" your performance (i.e., the MIDI data) in various ways, including in a "piano roll" or graphic editing style. This is a great way to check on your rhythmic timing, as most sequencers these days are accurate down to at least 1/480th of a quarter note! I find it very interesting to look at the screen and see where I might have been a little ahead or behind the beat. This can be a humbling experience, but it's a great way to tell if you're "in the pocket" rhythmically.

3) **Record your band while rehearsing or gigging.**

   I personally find that recording band rehearsals and gigs is very useful indeed. This not only helps you zero in on how your individual parts are working with the band, but also tells you how the band is sounding as a whole. In particular, recording rehearsals lets you iron out any trouble spots before the gig! Also, if you're in a cover or tribute band, you may want to record yourselves for comparison against the original artist's recordings (I have found this helpful for my Steely Dan tribute band here in Los Angeles). You don't want to obsess over small mistakes (which are not typically noticed by your adoring public), but you'll want to get an honest assessment of how you sound overall, and the recording doesn't lie!

# YIELD

If you are in a band, you should take every opportunity to *yield*: to listen to the other members in your group, and genuinely to interact with them (rather than playing in your "own little world" without being aware of the others). I have taught a lot of ensemble classes, and this is a common problem that I see in beginning-level players.

More experienced players will always be aware of their roles in the group, and what the other players are doing. If it's time for one of your bandmates to take a solo, then you should play a supportive role, and let him or her step into the spotlight. I find that volume and dynamics are often a problem with less experienced players (particularly in rock bands). Make sure you're not playing so loud that you're drowning out the other band members (although this problem probably applies more to guitarists than to keyboard players...!).

If you're always aware of your role in your band, and how you can make the band sound better as a whole, then other musicians will enjoy playing with you, and everybody wins!

# ZANY STUFF

One of the bands I perform with in the Los Angeles area is Doctor Wu, which is a fun Steely Dan tribute band. As you may know, Steely Dan (and in particular their keyboardist and main writer Donald Fagen) took elements of rock, jazz, and blues and forged a unique and identifiable style. Many of their keyboard parts are rather unconventional to say the least, so when I was thinking of ideas for this *Zany Stuff* section, I thought I would come up with a few grooves and phrases inspired by some famous Steely Dan and Donald Fagen songs. I hope you enjoy them!

TRACK 92
Part 1

"Greenflower Street"

This great fill consists of alternating B♭ major and E major triad arpeggios, over an E7 chord: not only a great lick, but a very good technical workout for the right hand!

TRACK 92
Part 2

"I Got the News" (1)

This fill is based on the C Mixolydian mode, used over a C7 chord. The first part uses Mixolydian triads, with sixteenth-note rhythms and syncopations. Then the triplet figure (alternating between a perfect 4th and a major 3rd) starts in bar 3, creating an interesting cross-rhythm against the left-hand part.

TRACK 92
Part 3

"I Got the News" (2)

This fill is based on the C eight-note dominant scale—introduced in *Eight-Note Scales* (p. 38). The sixteenth-note figure in the first measure (using octaves and minor 10ths between the hands) leads into a polychordal voicing in the second measure, with the right hand playing an E♭ minor triad (built from the sharped ninth of the C13 chord), over the left hand's double-4th shape E♮-B♭-E♭ ("3-7-#9" of C13).

**TRACK 92**
Part 4

"Jack of Speed"

This pattern uses A major and E major triads over the F#m7 chord (these triads are built from the third and seventh of the chord, respectively), within a funky sixteenth-note comping rhythm. At the end of the second measure, we have some rootless voicings for the E13 and G13 chords, with the left hand doubled an octave higher in the right.

**TRACK 92**
Part 5

"Babylon Sisters"

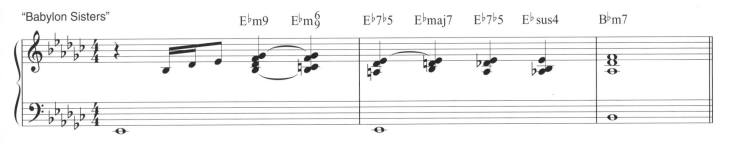

These chord voicings leading from the E♭m9 chord to the B♭m7 chord are quite unusual indeed! Check out the inner-voice motion by half steps as the chords move through the second measure.

**TRACK 92**
Part 6

"Kid Charlemagne"

C7#9

This comping groove on the C7#9 chord uses the double-4th shape E♮-B♭-E♭ ("3-7-#9" of the chord) in the right hand, with the grace note E♭ leading into the E♮. As an embellishment, this shape moves up by half step (to F-B-E) in the second measure. The left-hand sixteenth-note figure leading into the first beat of measure 2 comes from the C minor pentatonic scale.

TRACK 92
Part 7

"Josie"

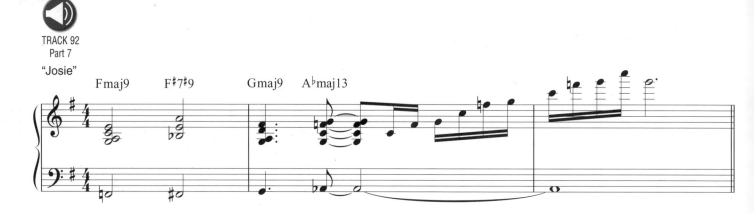

This chord sequence is voiced using upper-structure four-part and double-4th shapes in the right hand as follows:

- On the Fmaj9 chord we build a four-part minor seventh chord from the third: Am7/F.

- On the F#7#9 chord we build a double-4th shape ("3-7-#9") from the third.

- On the Gmaj9 chord we build a major triad from the fifth: D/G (with the root G also added in the right hand).

- On the Abmaj13 chord we build a double-4th shape ("7-3-13") from the seventh (and doubling the seventh on top). This shape is then played as an arpeggio from measure 2 into measure 3.

TRACK 92
Part 8

"My Old School"

In measures 1–2, the right hand is playing a cluster voicing (D-E-G) with the upper fingers while playing notes from the E blues scale underneath with the thumb. Then, in measure 3, we have whole steps and half steps (implying C major and C minor, respectively), leading into the unison octave riff derived from the G pentatonic/E blues scales in measures 4–5.